BELIEVE &
REJOICE

JAMES P. GILLS, M.D.

CREATION
HOUSE PRESS

BELIEVE AND REJOICE
By James P. Gills, M.D.
Published by Creation House Press
A Strang Company
600 Rinehart Road
Lake Mary, Florida 32746
www.creationhousepress.com

Unless otherwise noted, Scripture quotations are from the Holy Bible, New International Version. Copyright © 1973, 1978, 1984, International Bible Society. Used by permission.

Scripture quotations marked NKJV are from the New King James Version of the Bible. Copyright © 1979, 1980, 1982 by Thomas Nelson, Inc., publishers. Used by permission.

Cover design by Karen Grindley

Jesus Laughing, copyright © 1977 by Praise Screen Prints

www.jesuslaughing.com

Used with permission

Library of Congress Control Number: 2004105941
International Standard Book Number: 1-59185-608-6

04 05 06 07 08—987654321
Printed in the United States of America

This book is dedicated to all those who will grasp the inner joy that comes from faithfully relinquishing themselves to God. Our daughters are named Joy, Peace (Shea), and Charity. This book is dedicated to those three names and those three people. When a relinquished life becomes faithful to the promises of God, the result is His joy, His peace, and His charity. Our daughters' names are symbols of the results of a relinquished life that believes totally in the promises of God.

To this we dedicate all our labors: to the future generations that will follow Him in a relinquished and faithful manner, trusting in His grace with an outpouring of joy, peace, and charity.

—JAMES P. GILLS AND GARY CARTER

ACKNOWLEDGMENTS

THIS book would not have been possible without my good friend and colleague at St. Luke's, Gary Carter. Gary and I have spent countless hours studying, discussing, praying, and fellowshiping over God's Word and its meaning in our lives. Gary is truly filled with faith in God's promises, and I am blessed to share in his life of joy.

I would also like to thank the staff members at St. Luke's Cataract & Laser Institute, especially Lois Babcock, for generously providing their encouragement and direction, and Vicotria Krueger for her editing assitance.

And finally, my thanks to my wife, Heather. Her love and insight continue to be a source of inspiration to me.

CONTENTS

Introduction 1

  1 A Heart of Faith, A Life of Joy 5

  2 The Joy of Salvation 9

  3 Being Relinquished 13

  4 Traits of a Relinquished Life 27

  5 The Struggle to Stay Relinquished 33

  6 Relinquished or Religious? 45

  7 Restored to Joy 53

  8 Worship and Joy 57

  9 A Joyous Life 69

 10 Joy and Peace 75

Verses About Joy 81

Verses About Worship 85

Relinquished Heart or Religious Spirit? 89

Scripture Index 97

Notes 99

INTRODUCTION

DURING an interesting part of my life in which there were a lot of temptations and trials, I read a short little book by the Reverend Henry Scougal called *The Life of God in the Soul of Man.*[1] I read this book ten times because it meant so much to me during that time. And each time I read it, its message became more and more meaningful.

This book showed me how my life can be filled with joy. All I had to do was really believe in God, always be dependent on Him, and always worship Him. Then my trials and temptations would be overshadowed by His love for me and my joy in resting in Him. John 3:16 is the verse that simply says we are resting in His redemption. Oswald Chambers said that all prayer that isn't based on resting in His redemption is foolishness. "For God so loved the world that He gave His only begotten Son, that whoever believes in Him should not perish but have everlasting life" (John 3:16, NKJV) simply says that God loves us, He is the one who saves us, and we are going to rest in that and live. That's the essence of the Christian walk.

The Psalmist explains it so beautifully this way:

> Whom have I in heaven but you? And earth has nothing I desire
> besides you. My flesh and my heart may fail, but God is the
> strength of my heart and my portion forever.
> —PSALM 73:25–26

In the final analysis, we have no one but our Creator, the Lord God, and He is all we will ever need. The God who set the universe in motion also concerns Himself with the daily needs in each of our lives. And all we have to do is trust in the Savior's work on the cross and embrace His control of our lives, acknowledge His majesty and greatness, believe in His promises, and live in a loving relationship with Him. And in that relationship we find joy.

Communion with the risen Lord is our daily joy; this is the source of our strength in all that we do. How can we be anything but joyful when we experience a close relationship with the Creator of the universe, enjoying His peace and presence forever? For when we believe in Him and surrender ourselves to His will, we are filled with a joyful spirit. We must do all the things we do because of God's love, not to obtain God's love. Then there will be a natural outpouring of joy.

> These things I have spoken to you, that My joy may remain in
> you, and that your joy may be full.
> —JOHN 15:11, NKJV

> As the Father loved Me, I also have loved you; abide in My
> love.
> —JOHN 15:9, NKJV

We must abide in His love and do everything because God loves us. This is set before us in that wonderful passage, Ephesians 3:17–19, NKJV:

> That Christ may dwell in your hearts through faith; that you,
> being roted and grounded in love, may be able to comprehend
> with all the saints what is the width and length and depth and
> height—to know the love of Christ which passes knowledge;
> that you may be filled with all the fullness of God.

The Reverend Scougal writes that we cannot have this true joy of God until we have surrendered everything—our wants, our desires, our anger, our resentment, and our bitterness—to Him. Eighteenth century theologian and evangelist Jonathan Edwards called this surrender "religious affections." By that he meant we are not just surrendered; our hearts are engaged fervently in praising and worshiping God because His Word has come to us with power and we believe in Him. The Bible teaches us that He wants our praise because we have received His salvation, and we enjoy His fellowship.

And then we are transformed. When we are filled with these "holy affections," our lives are no longer an endless search for meaning. We surrender ourselves, putting the focus of our lives on God and on worshiping Him. We are filled with the presence of God. Indeed, we must relinquish ourselves to God in faith or we will never be able to worship and love Him fully.

And we will never have a completely joyous existence unless we worship Him with a heart that fervently believes in Him.

Believing God's promises, not just intellectually but also in the inner being, has transformed people and nations. That kind of belief grabs everything about us and changes our lives.

When we praise Him, we are filled with joy. That joy strengthens us in daily life, in our service, and in our work for God. When I do not have God's joy, the day is very long, and I am less effective. When I have His joy, the day is easy.

Daily I have to examine myself and make sure I am receiving His Word and resting in His love. I trust in God and relinquish control to Him. I let my relationship with Him govern the rest of my life. I must rest in His presence, not wrestle for control with Him. Then, when my heart is given over to Him in faith I am naturally filled with joy. This joy is not something I can seek. It happens only because He is at work in me, and I believe in Him. He is in charge, and our relationship is in order.

What all this means to me is that life is too short not to be full of joy! Life is too short to be jealous or envious of others. It is too short to be angry or resentful. It is too short to carry a grudge. It is too short to worry about material goods and be caught up in the pursuit of status or possessions. It is too short to do anything other than trust in Him, worship Him, and let His joy fill my life.

Explore with me in this book how we can relinquish our hearts to God, believing in Him, worshiping Him, and enjoying Him forever—for a joy-filled life in Him!

CHAPTER 1

A HEART OF FAITH,
A LIFE OF JOY

Glory in his holy name; let the hearts of those
who seek the LORD rejoice.

—1 CHRONICLES 16:10

THINK about the word *joy*. What image comes to mind?
Angels in the heavens announcing the birth of Christ? A
child full of laughter and happiness? Beethoven's beautiful
Ninth Symphony? Nineteenth century preacher C. H. Spurgeon said,
"Joy is peace dancing." What a wonderful image!

God wants us to have a life filled with more joy than we can ever
imagine. It doesn't happen by accident, but it does surprise us. Author
C. S. Lewis writes that we find joy only when we are looking for something else.[1] And that something else is God. It is a one-two punch: we
seek God, really believing in Him, and we find joy. Lewis says it more
eloquently: joy is the response or result of the felt sense of God's love
in our soul.

It is a journey we undertake when we turn our lives over to God.
When we truly believe in God, we surrender every worry, every concern, every aspect of our lives to Him. We are concerned only about
living in God's presence and believing in His promises.

The apostle Paul describes three critical steps in this journey to a
joy-filled life: relinquishment, faith, and grace.

> I have been crucified with Christ and I no longer live, but Christ lives in me. The life I live in the body, I live by faith in the Son of God, who loved me and gave Himself for me.
>
> —Galatians 2:20

Sometimes we are reluctant to talk about joy and God. We tend to associate joy with comfort, ease, and luxury. But joy is a much deeper and richer experience. It is the natural outpouring of our hearts as God's presence becomes the central pillar of our lives. When we have a personal relationship with Him, we cannot help but be filled with infinite, glorious joy and the desire to worship and adore God. His full presence in our lives is the ultimate joy.

How do we get that kind of personal relationship? First, we have to acknowledge God as our Creator. Then we have to really believe in Him as our Savior. We have to love Him and trust Him enough to give Him control of our lives. There is an old-fashioned word to describe it—relinquishment. The dictionary says that to relinquish means to abandon, surrender, let go. When we are passengers in a car, we have to relinquish control to the person behind the wheel or we are terrible backseat drivers.

For Christians, relinquishing means surrendering our lives, giving up our wants and desires, cares and worries, abandoning our selfish nature, and receiving God's love, trusting His provision, and experiencing His filling. Our faith helps us leave behind all the cares and concerns of this world. We can call it "abandoned faith" because we are abandoning the world for a life of faith in God. We are filled with trust in God, and we relinquish control to Him. And then we are filled with abundant, glorious joy.

The experience of John Wesley, the great evangelist and founder of the Methodist movement, shows how abandoned faith can change a life. By the time he was thirty-five, Wesley knew a lot about Christ. He had been to Oxford and was an ordained priest in the Church of England. He and his brother, Charles, helped start the Holy Club at Oxford. He read one hundred spiritual books a year for a dozen years. And he even traveled to Georgia on a mission trip. But he knew there was something missing. On his mission trip he met some Moravian immigrants who had the spiritual peace he realized he was lacking. His work in America was not very effective, and he returned to England.

Back in London, Wesley met Peter Böhler, a Moravian who convinced him that what he needed was simple: he needed faith, not just knowledge. During a meeting in Aldersgate Street in 1738, Wesley was transformed. As he heard Martin Luther's preface to the Commentary on Romans being read, he was truly elated. He realized the promises of God are true! He wrote, "I felt my heart strangely warmed. I felt I did trust in Christ, Christ alone, for salvation." He felt a quickening that comes from truly experiencing God's grace and presence. He was filled with God's complete and perfect joy.

From this point on, Wesley was a changed man. He preached with a spiritual fire and fervor that was fed by his faith. And he was filled with a glorious joy that affected him the rest of his life because he was relinquished to God and believed in His promises.

We can have the same kind of life filled with abandoned faith and joy. It's a faith and joy that comes from inner harmony. There is no internal struggle, no complaining about trouble, no worries about trying to control the future. When we believe in God's promises and trust Him to be in control of our lives, joy is the glorious result. We do not have joy; it has us. Our joy in God is based on His delight in us. (See Psalm 149:4.)

What an offer! If we quit worrying about our own lives and trust God to do the driving, we will find our lives full of blessings and riches beyond our wildest dreams. Indeed, we cannot even begin to know all the blessings we will receive. And we limit God when we try.

> Indeed, if we consider the unblushing promises of reward and the staggering nature of the rewards promised in the Gospels, it would seem that our Lord finds our desires not too strong, but too weak. We are half-hearted creatures, fooling about with drink and sex and ambition when infinite joy is offered us, like an ignorant child who wants to go on making mud pies in a slum because he cannot imagine what is meant by the offer of a holiday at the sea. We are far too easily pleased. We accept what is much less for what could be more.[2]

In this study, through our reading, exploration of the Word, and prayer together, that is what we will find—the infinite, glorious joy that results from believing in God.

Dear Lord Jesus, bless us as we discover Your truths and learn to love You as You love us.

CHAPTER TWO

THE JOY OF SALVATION

The LORD your God is with you, he is mighty
to save. He will take great delight in you, he will
quiet you with his love, he will rejoice over you
with singing.

—ZEPHANIAH 3:17

EACH of us has struggled to find joy, thinking the "right" thing
in our work, our play, or our relationships will fulfill us. We
create such hectic days full of activities and accomplishments
that we think a filled life is a fulfilled life. We seek recreations on a
basketball court, a gym, or a bicycle that engage us for the moment
but are not lasting. Or we search for that "special someone," only to
discover that our problem is not in finding the right person, but that
we are not the right person ourselves.

C. S. Lewis says that each of us has this kind of deep longing that
we search to fill. He calls it *sehnsucht* or "longing for joy." Because we
are human, we try to fill it with earthly things.

We say, "If I can just get my education finished and get started
in my career, then things will go well and I will be happy." But we
are not happy. So we say, "If I can just get established in my business and be successful, then things will go well and I will be happy."
But it doesn't happen. Then we think, "Well, if I can just find the
right spouse and have good children, then things will go well and I
will be happy." But that still doesn't satisfy us. So then we say, "If
I can just get the kids through school, then I can settle down and

9

rest." But we are missing the point.

There are no magic plateaus where our lives level off and we think we have achieved happiness. Personal achievements, success at work or on the athletic field, and relationships cannot give us lasting joy. We can have all those things and still feel this empty longing.

At some point in our lives we have to realize that what we seek isn't within ourselves; we lack the inner resources to fill this void. We finally see how weak we are, how limited are our powers. We can be eaten up with despair, frustration, anger, anxiety, and loneliness.

Then God speaks to us. For the first time, we truly begin to see the power and majesty of the Almighty God. We see ourselves as poor, needy sinners who need the grace of the Lord Jesus and His cross. We turn to God because we realize we have nowhere else to go.

> For it is by grace you have been saved, through faith—and this is not from yourselves, it is the gift of God—not by works, so that no one can boast.
>
> —EPHESIANS 2:8–9

Paul tells us in these verses, first, that God's grace saves us, and then, that God has a plan for our lives, as a physician or nurse, a teacher, a mechanic, a firefighter, a politician, a husband, or a wife.

Our concept of grace varies immensely with our experiences over the course of our lives. We never quite fully understand it. We may delight in it, we may cry over it, we may laugh over it, and we may worship over it.

But we know that the power of grace can conquer the temptations in our lives and many other problems that destroy us.

God wants us to have a relinquished spirit that has faith in His grace. If we have anything other than that, we are not being true to Him.

Jonathan Edwards said it so beautifully:

> If you're a poor distressed sinner whose heart is ready to sink for fear that God never will have mercy on you, you need not be afraid to go to Christ, for fear that he is either unable or unwilling to help you. Here is a strong foundation, inexhaustible treasure, to answer the necessities of your poor soul, and here is infinite grace and gentleness to invite you to come boldly, poor

unworthy fearful soul, to come into it.[1]

How gracious and sweet is the invitation to be with Him. We fall at His feet and say, "Lord, I'm a poor, worthless sinner. Please, in your everlasting mercy and grace, accept me, take me, let me be Yours. Be my Redeemer, Savior and Friend, for in you I trust and believe and love."

Then our souls are flooded with the joy of salvation. We begin to see the infinite majesty of God. He has given us hope and joy in believing.

> Then my soul will rejoice in the LORD and delight in his salvation.
>
> —PSALM 35:9

Joy is a heart that is changed by knowing God. It takes our breath away. It is an infinite host of angels singing glory to God. It is the greatest music or words we can ever imagine, and still more. This great joy puts everything else out of our heads and our hearts. In turning from earthly things we find God. And by putting our faith in Him, we are filled with abundant joy.

If you have not accepted Jesus as your personal Savior and Friend, pray with me:

> *Lord, I realize how far short I have fallen. I know I'm not worthy of Your love. But, through the miracle of Your grace, forgive me and make me Your child. Help me turn to You and love You. Show me how to live and love and be like You.*

CHAPTER 3

BEING RELINQUISHED

W E cannot have joy without love. It is like two people in love—joy springs up and fills them when they have an unconditional love for each other. That is the joy that should be our response to Christ—someone who loves us far more than anyone else ever could.

This new relationship has a wonderful sense of love and joy. The Bible calls it delight. "For the Lord takes delight in his people" (Ps. 149:4). God takes pleasure in us; we rejoice in that and take pleasure in Him. We are joyful in our King.

Love is essential to a life of faith and joy. God's Word tells us just how important it is:

> Love the LORD your God with all your heart and with all your soul and with all your strength.
> —DEUTERONOMY 6:5

Now, some people believe Christians are those who are truly blessed, but their hearts are so full of hurt and doubt that they cannot love. These people find loving Christ is impossible. Even some who would like to love Him avoid it. They put on only a superficial show of true love and commitment because of past hurts.

For any of us, love must be a key step to a life that is surrendered in faith to God. Without love, our actions and words are meaningless. First Corinthians 13 says it like this: we can have the gift of prophecy, understand all mysteries and knowledge, have faith to move mountains, give all our goods to the poor, and have our body burned. And we can have all sorts of abilities to speak, but unless we are relinquished in love to Christ and others, all these gifts and abilities do us no good.

As we tell God He is wonderful, we are in love with Him. It is like a marriage. As I tell my wife that she is wonderful, I am in love with her. Look at couples who struggle in their marriages. Insecurities, pride, hostility and many other forms of selfishness keep them from becoming close and surrendering to one another.

We have the same problems in our relationship with Christ. We all have anxieties, frustrations, and doubts. But God asks us to let Him have them. He asks us to love Him and be in communion with Him. A heart filled with love has less room for selfishness. As we love God more and more, we can relinquish ourselves more and more.

We need to be able to look up to Jesus by faith and say, "Jesus, you're wonderful. I love You and I am Your child—Your spiritual child, Your child for eternity."

SWEET SURRENDER

If we are really going to be committed to God, we have to be committed to living a life that honors Him. We have to be able to say, "Lord, You're in charge now. I put all my faith in You. You lead; I'll follow." We must give up our worldly agendas and desires and trust His control of our lives. Then we find joy not by worldly standards—success, fame, money, power. We find it in the outpouring of the love of our Creator and Redeemer into our hearts. (See Romans 5:5.) Then we pour out our love to Him.

Think about it again like a marriage. I love my wife. I want what she wants; I sacrifice for her. I surrender myself to the joy of knowing, caring, and appreciating her. I love to pray with my wife. One verse we pray together repeats what Adam said of Eve: "This is now bone of my bones and flesh of my flesh" (Gen. 2:23). That helps us remember that we can't really become one person, one partnership living in harmony, until we relinquish ourselves.

And just as any of us surrender to our spouses, so we must surrender ourselves to our God. We become one with God as we totally surrender and are integrated with Him—the flesh of his flesh, the bone of his bone.

We love and trust God so completely that we can surrender our lives to Him. Love gives us the strength and trust to turn everything over to Him. Remember Paul's road map in Galatians 2:20 for this journey: surrender, faith, and grace. Let's look again at this first part:

> I have been crucified with Christ and I no longer live, but Christ lives in me.

What Paul says so beautifully is that we cannot live in Christ until we are ready to die to self—our own wants, desires and egos. Jesus says it this way:

> Then he said to them all: "If anyone would come after me, he must deny himself and take up his cross daily and follow me. For whoever wants to save his life will lose it, but whoever loses his life for me will save it."
>
> —LUKE 9:23–24

> I tell you the truth, unless a kernel of wheat falls to the ground and dies, it remains only a single seed. But if it dies, it produces many seeds. The man who loves his life will lose it, while the man who hates his life in this world will keep it for eternal life.
>
> —JOHN 12:24–25

Paul also writes about relinquishment:

> I die every day—I mean that, brothers—just as surely as I glory over you in Christ Jesus our Lord.
>
> —1 CORINTHIANS 15:31

> We always carry around in our body the death of Jesus, so that the life of Jesus may also be revealed in our body.
>
> —2 CORINTHIANS 4:10

We must die to ourselves before we can truly appreciate God. We must give up our egos and all that goes with them—pride and the desire for control, worldly status and success. This is what it means to be born again of the Spirit. And we must make our bodies full of abandonments and living sacrifices wholly acceptable unto God. The world and all of its lures, temptations, and struggles no longer have a grip on our lives. We belong to God and He lives in us. The Bible warns us about the opposite attitude:

> Don't you know that friendship with the world is hatred toward God? Anyone who chooses to be a friend of the world becomes an enemy of God.
>
> —JAMES 4:4

Everybody knows you must take risks to be successful by earthly standards. What we risk in order to make anything spiritually of our lives is even greater. We have to risk worldly success, risk losing our feeling of independence, risk giving up control of our lives. But what we gain is so great, the risks pale in comparison. Charles Swindoll asks, "Are you willing to risk as much to make a difference as you are willing to risk to make a dollar?"[1] To be truly relinquished we have to risk it all.

As the apostle Paul wrote:

> I consider everything a loss compared to the surpassing greatness of knowing Christ Jesus my Lord, for whose sake I have lost all things. I consider them rubbish, that I may gain Christ and be found in him.
>
> —PHILIPPIANS 3:8–9

Dear God, we love You so very much. Help us to lovingly surrender all the parts and pieces of our lives to You, that we may honor and glorify Your name above all others.

FAITH: THE SIXTH SENSE

The life I live in the body, I live by faith in the Son of God.
—GALATIANS 2:20

Great athletes must forget about everything else so they can train and play wholeheartedly. If they worry about getting injured or worry about how other athletes are doing, they cannot perform well. They cannot focus.

That is the essence of abandoned faith to the Lord: giving everything wholeheartedly to Him—every worry, concern, desire, and goal. It is a faith that is not just in our minds; it is a faith that believes all the promises of God. We must have a total abandonment spiritually, totally trusting in the Lord. The joy in our hearts that comes from abandonment to Him keeps us from worrying about the cares of the day, the politics of the day, and the cynicism of the day. It lets us be concerned only about being totally abandoned and surrendered to the Lord.

The apostle Paul, Martin Luther, and John Wesley are just some of the great Christians who went through a time when they truly had to believe. They knew all about the promises of God. But they didn't know Him. Someone explained it so simply and beautifully to Wesley, "Preach faith until you have faith. Believing is the essence."

Let's look at the word belief. Hebrews 11:6 tells us to diligently seek God, emphasizing that belief isn't simply an intellectual exercise. Instead, we lean upon, abide in, draw strength from, and become one with belief, and we act the way we believe.

Faith is really a sixth sense. The first five senses—touch, taste, smell, hearing, and sight—are in carnal man. The sixth sense is in the spiritual man. The carnal man can't appreciate faith any more than the sense of hearing appreciates the sense of smell.

But the sixth sense is absolutely essential if we are going to live complete lives full of joy. In seeking God, faith is given to us as we hear His Word.

> Consequently, faith comes from hearing the message, and the
> message is heard through the word of Christ.
> —ROMANS 10:17

The battle we have with our carnal selves is won in our hearts with God when we believe in Him. Then we step into a life of faith. And when we fully believe in God and His promises, then we have an abandoned faith that focuses on God and forgets the world.

Look at the example of Robert Morrison. He was one of the first missionaries to China in the early 1800s. As he was sailing to China, the captain of the ship asked, rather sarcastically, "So, Mr. Morrison, you expect to make an impression on the great empire of China, do you?" Morrison replied, "No, I expect God will."[2] What a shining example of believing God's promises! Morrison served twenty-seven years in China, and he is considered the father of Protestant mission work there.

It doesn't take a great mind or years of education to have such abandoned faith. As the old hymn says, "Trust and obey, for there's no other way." All each of us needs to do is trust in God and believe in His promises.

However, we can either believe in the right things or the wrong things. What are some of those deceptions we can start believing? "Life should be fair." "My unhappiness is because of someone else." "My good is determined by what I can do." "Our marriage requires too much work; we must not be right for each other." We start believing there are certain things we can do or things we can own that will solve our problems and fill our longings. But when we start seeking things that are not focused on God, we no longer have abandoned faith in Him. Instead, we start to abandon our faith in His promises.

We need not be deceived by the difficult times in our lives. God promises to help us through them. All we need to believe is that His grace is sufficient and all our blessings come because we believe in Him.

> *Dear Father, thank You for being so good to us. May our faith and trust in You grow daily.*

COMMUNION AND CONVERSATION

When we love God, we want to be in His presence, and we want to be able to talk with Him and share ourselves with Him. Prayer is one way we can be in constant communion with Him. In prayer we make the nearest approach to God. It opens the inward thoughts of both God and man, and true intimacy is found. In true sincerity we must open our hearts to God in prayer: sometimes with thoughtful, eloquent prayers, sometimes with words that cannot be uttered, sometimes with thoughts that cannot be translated. And then our hearts and our total beings are surrendered in intimacy to Him.

Fervent and hearty prayer is necessary. Daylong prayers are necessary. This life of prayer should be a state of meditation on the glory of God. We must have this kind of personal, vital relationship with Him. Otherwise Christianity becomes a joyless burden, and the only thing we will regret is that we didn't pray because we didn't relinquish ourselves and have faith in His grace.

This intimacy through prayer leads to fulfillment of joy because prayer is the nerve center of our vital fellowship with Jesus. It brings us a life filled with deep, abiding joy. As 1 John 1:3–4 says, "Our fellowship is with the Father and with his Son, Jesus Christ. We write this to make our joy complete."

We measure fluids by gallons. We measure a dog's value by how much an owner is willing to pay a veterinarian for the dog's health care. God measures us by our prayer life. Our value is determined by our prayer life both now and evermore—how we praise God, how we come close to God, how it helps us to be transformed into His image.

We become what we love and honor. One way to show that love and honor is through prayer. That gives us all we need for today—peace and joy—and for eternity.

Father, let us love You, and in love, surrender to You, to Your grace, to Your will, with the help of the Holy Spirit, filling us with Your presence.

THE HELP OF THE HOLY SPIRIT

No matter how much we try to will ourselves to surrender everything to God, it is something we cannot do alone. In a marriage our spouses help us. To be truly relinquished to God, we need the Holy Spirit working in us. C. H. Spurgeon said, "There are times when I've been a half-inch from heaven and you've been a half-inch from heaven."[3] The Holy Spirit makes that difference as we focus on Him and wait on Him for His Spirit and His closeness. His *Shekinah* glory, the manifested glory of God, fills us, displacing the rest of the world. Then we are able to empty ourselves of the world and fill ourselves with Him.

Moses gives us a vivid example of a life filled with this kind of glory:

When Moses came down from Mount Sinai with the two tablets of the Testimony in his hands, he was not aware that his face was radiant because he had spoken with the LORD. When Aaron and all the Israelites saw Moses, his face was radiant, and they were afraid to come near him. But Moses called to them; so Aaron and all the leaders of the community came back to him, and he spoke to them…When Moses finished speaking to them, he put a veil over his face. But whenever he entered the LORD's presence to speak with him, he removed the veil until he came out. And when he came out and told the Israelites what he had been commanded, they saw that his face was radiant. Then Moses would put the veil back over his face until he went in to speak with the LORD.

—EXODUS 34:29–31, 33–35

Moses had that physical reflection of the Shekinah glory because he was so close to the Lord that he radiated with the glory of the Lord. And those around him would be alarmed by the glorious radiance of the Lord's presence. The Shekinah glory is not something just for Old Testament prophets, however. It is available to all of us today as we seek His presence.

For God, who said, "Let light shine out of darkness," made his light shine in our hearts to give us the light of the knowledge of the glory of God in the face of Christ.

—2 CORINTHIANS 4:6

And that glory comes through the Holy Spirit. John 1:4 says that in Jesus "was life, and that life was the light of men." So Jesus, as the Light of life, through the Holy Spirit, gives light upon the holy things of God. We need to have God, Jesus, and the Holy Spirit all wrapped together to give us the joy that results from being present with Him. Shekinah glory comes only when we have a relinquished spirit that loves Him, cares for Him, and worships Him. Then His Shekinah glory is present within us, radiating into us and out into the world.

I have worked with nurses who had an aura of radiance. They might not have said anything holy, but their lives were filled with the presence of the Holy Spirit. They were full of the love of God and were completely surrendered to Him, letting Him direct their lives. This spirit of joy, peace, and thanksgiving is truly a wonderful sight.

I have felt a similar glow in my life. I will first mention that I am not much of an athlete, but I did fairly well years ago at a Double Iron Triathlon. At that time, I was fifty-six. I came in one minute behind the first American, who was twenty-eight, finishing in about twenty-seven hours. I did it that day just by prayer. USA Today and other newspapers wrote about the event, but no one wrote that during the whole event I was in one of those glows that many of us experience. The presence of the Holy Spirit throughout the race kept me going. I was at my peak through the whole event; I was never down. It probably was my best athletic achievement ever. And it was due not to my own strength, but to God. "The joy of the Lord is your strength" (Neh. 8:10)!

The Israelites discovered that truth in the Old Testament. When they came out of their captivity in Babylon, they had nothing but the Word of God. When they heard it, they understood it and went their way rejoicing. They understood that though they had no material goods they should not grieve and mourn. To be in God's presence is joyous and completely filling. The Israelites restored the Feast of Tabernacles, a feast of thanksgiving that honors God as the host and the Israelites as the guests.

In the same way, we daily should come to the Word of God and rejoice in His presence because we have faith in Him and in His Spirit.

The radiance of the Holy Spirit lets everyone see that we are truly His. It enables us to reflect Christ and His love. We can be like the nurses with that holy aura. They don't need to speak. They just let the light of Christ shine in their lives. The Holy Spirit can permeate the lives of each of us, so we will think differently, act differently, live differently.

We can describe the smile of God upon our hearts that allows us to speak His Word.[4] He uses the word unction. This is God's holiness speaking through us. Jesus' disciples set an example of this unction:

> And the disciples were filled with joy and with the Holy Spirit.
> —Acts 13:52

The disciples were infused with this joy in the Holy Spirit because their hearts were joined to God and filled with His presence. A few verses earlier we learn that when the Gentiles heard the good news of the gospel, they rejoiced, praising and honoring the Word of God, and they were glorified. (See Acts 13:48.) They were filled with joy because it came from the praise of the Holy Spirit. And that praise changes our inner being and gives us true joy. When the Holy Spirit gives us His glory, we need to enjoy it and cherish it, and tell Him how wonderful He is to give it to us.

Tony Evans describes the importance of the Holy Spirit in the believer's life in a surprising manner.[4] His analogy is jumper cables from Jesus to us. Can you imagine having jumper cables to use in the morning to get your mind turned on right? Jumper cables for feeling the promises of God are true for your whole being. They are jumper cables that really make us feel that Jesus is within us by the power of the Holy Spirit. Tony's example of the Holy Spirit is just one of the many examples of how God works in us when we give ourselves to be abandoned to Him and seek the Holy Spirit to work through us. All of this is to one end: to glorify Him and to live with Him in love, enjoying Him and glorifying Him forever.

> May the God of hope fill you with all joy and peace as you trust in him, so that you may overflow with hope by the power of the Holy Spirit.
>
> —ROMANS 15:13

FINDING FELICITY

Felicity was a servant saint who lived around the year 200 AD. She was executed because she refused to renounce her belief in God. Even when she was put in an arena with a wild bull, she did not deny Christ, but died praising Him. Hers is a story of a girl who desired God above all things.

Felicity teaches us that it is impossible to have God's ultimate joy if we do not truly believe and trust in Him. That attitude can be called felicity—God's tranquility personified. Felicity, the saint, had that presence within her. We should seek the same thing. Her faith in God and love for Him set a shining example for us today.

When we relinquish ourselves to God, we rest in the peace that He will be Jehovah Jireh—the Great Provider of all. (See Genesis 22:14.) We have felicity, His tranquility. This attitude of felicity is not only satisfaction, peace, and joy; it is evidence that we are in right standing with God, that we are subduing our sinful nature. Then the things of the world will be put in the proper perspective, and we will enjoy them more because we are aligned with Him.

The felicity we receive from God is one that is filling and satisfying. The satisfactions we try to get from the world—material goods, admiration, and respect from others, sensual pleasures—in the long run leave us with the greatest emptiness. We think they will satisfy us, but they never live up to our expectations. The emptiness that follows is overwhelming and leads to the greatest despair, even when we have gotten everything we wanted. When the football players in the Super Bowl win that championship ring—something they have sought for their whole careers—there can be the greatest emptiness in the center of that ring if that victory is not from God. True felicity and satisfaction are not present in the world; they are present only in knowing Christ.

St. Augustine said, "Love God, and do what you want." We become like God when we love Him with all of our heart. Therefore if we love our heavenly Father we will want to please Him. We see that St. Augustine was setting forth the basic principle of the heart. What is it that rules in our hearts? Is it love to God? God's Word tells us what love to God is like. So when we love God we will seek to do what God's Word says. (See 1 John 5:3.) It is important that we feel God's love for us. So when we are dull of heart we need to seek Him to rekindle in our hearts that sense of His great love for us.

How does this apply to our everyday life? For years I have been involved in the Department of Ophthalmology at the University of South Florida in Tampa. I am a clinical professor there, and I am on the board that selected the head of the department. I chose Dr. James Rowsey to come here from Oklahoma City.

Jim is an outstanding man. He is brilliant, pleasant, and delightful. As much as anyone I know, he exhibits the joy of God. He has also gotten into trouble. He has been sued because he prays for patients, and he has been sued by people who work for him because they thought he was partial to other employees who are Christians. When Jim was sued by the ACLU he realized that many of the ACLU attorneys do not believe in God. Jim realized that God loves the attorneys of the ACLU also. The difference was that Jim believed and embraced God's love. One of the great lessons he learned was that it was essential for the one who knows God's love to pray for those who do not know it. He has always had to face difficulties because of his Christian commitment, but his joy in knowing Jesus just overcomes the problems.

What has he done? He was able to revive a department that was dying. It came alive again; he reopened the eye center there. He has done it all on one foundation—the joy of the Lord. His joy is sincere and genuine. It comes from knowing who Christ is. This joy is meek and humble and beautiful.

It is also very effective. Dr. Rowsey influences everyone around him. He has Jewish people and people from all over the Arab world working with him, and he is able to influence them. He is a person who stands strongly for his Christian faith.

Richard Baxter, a seventeenth century theologian, noted that love, desire, hope and courage lead us to a joy in God. He said these emotions, these affections or influences over the heart, flow from our innermost being after we praise God and find there the excellence of Christ. Then we turn away and find that external joys mean nothing without Christ in them.

We call it "enlarging the neck" because these affections basically make an opening between the head and heart. Everything we think about we contemplate in godly ways, and those things become part of our heart and permeate our whole body. While it's important to think about these things, it is also important to feel them. We cannot only make logic within our head; we must praise with our heart.

A person's heart is the source of his or her joy. Everything must promote that joy. It is necessary for the heart to elevate the soul in what Baxter called "heavenly contemplations." We must love and be loved. Then we feel this felicity, this afterglow, this all-desiring emotion of being close to God.

Felicity varies within us because we are not always totally committed to the Lord. For heaven knows that all of us have let our thoughts and our actions become sinful, and we have lost God's felicity and tranquility. There are times when we are so full of everything in life that is not of felicity. We are filled with the things of the world, and we are taken away from our fellowship with the Lord. Remembering the times of felicity brings us back to Him. We are restored and no longer travel the road that leads to further deceit and hurt.

So often we have wandered along and contented ourselves with vain shadows and false imaginations of piety and religion, not truly believing in His promises. The affections that lead to felicity are stirred by more divine impressions and touched by our faith in Him.

Lord, help us to open our eyes and see that our whole purpose is to love You and enjoy You forever in a state of felicity.

CHAPTER 4

TRAITS OF A RELINQUISHED LIFE

A UTHOR C. S. Lewis described joy as a "meaningful acceleration, a rhythm with the character of God."[1] We don't sit still. We physically and mentally become more and more involved in the character of God because we are surrendered to Him. Let's go back to Galatians 2:20. It says, "I no longer live, but Christ lives in me." This means we want what God wants. We become more and more like Him.

Have you ever been around a couple who have been married a long time? Their marriage has transformed them. They have become like each other. In fact, sometimes they finish each other's sentences because they are of one mind and heart. There is a harmony between them. Their love for each other fills them with joy, peace, gentleness, and goodness. And that attitude carries over into their relationships with other people. Their loving relationship has truly united them.

When we relinquish ourselves in faith to God, we have a divine life through our Lord and Savior. Our surrendered hearts find joy in the Lord, and our lives are filled with the same qualities as that married couple—love, joy, peace, patience, kindness, goodness, faithfulness, gentleness, and self-control. (See Galatians 5:22–23.) This fruit of the

Holy Spirit changes us, and our relationships with others change.

As we stand close to God, His image is stamped on us. We are transformed. It cannot be any other way. We have to be changed because the Holy Spirit lives in us.

> Do not conform any longer to the pattern of this world, but be transformed by the renewing of your mind. Then you will be able to test and approve what God's will is—his good, pleasing and perfect will.
>
> —ROMANS 12:2

Our being must be transformed from the inside out. Our old thought processes are destroyed, and we are renewed by His Word, through prayer and worship, encouraging the Spirit. Our lives are changed through faith and surrender to God. Let's look at some of the changes that occur as we give our hearts and minds to God.

THE ETERNAL VIEW

As an ophthalmologist, I see a lot of people who are nearsighted. They only see the things that are up close. All of us can be nearsighted spiritually, seeing only the things that are up close in ourselves and in those around us. We can fail to see the overall view. James 4:14 describes this nearsightedness, "Why, you do not even know what will happen tomorrow. What is your life? You are a mist that appears for a little while and then vanishes."

That is the way we are if we don't relinquish our lives with the help of the Holy Spirit. When we are selfish and caught up in our own daily dramas, we cannot truly see. When we believe in His promises, our focus is no longer on the things of this world. We see the distant view—the eternity, the greatness of all reality. That is when we begin to comprehend who God really is.

Remember Psalm 73:25? "Whom have I in heaven but you? And earth has nothing I desire besides you." When our hearts are relinquished to God through the Holy Spirit, we no longer put our faith in our own abilities, but we trust in God. Isaiah 2:22 says, "Stop trusting in man, who has but a breath in his nostrils. Of what account is he?"

When we are centered on God, we have a fuller, deeper understanding of ourselves and we are able to worship Him for His power and majesty. As we stand close to Him, the things of this world are put in proper perspective, and we can truly enjoy them as we align ourselves with Him.

By relinquishing ourselves to God, we hand over our egos, our independence, our desires and our worries about the future. It is not easy to give up this control. As human beings we like to be in charge of our lives. And the world tells us that we should be in control. But when we see through God's eyes, we know He will provide for us and we trust implicitly in Him.

As we struggle with this battle for control of our lives, remember these words:

> Trust in the LORD with all your heart and lean not on your own understanding; in all your ways acknowledge him, and he will make your paths straight.
>
> —PROVERBS 3:5–6

PEACE AND FELICITY

Let's look at a rubber band. It is either at ease or stretched. And if it is stretched too tightly, it can break. We frequently are like a stretched rubber band. We are at the breaking point because we are busy trying to do things by our own power. And when we are trying to be in control, basically we are caught up in sin. At that point we are stretched and tense like an over-extended rubber band. We are not at peace, and we do not have the joy that comes from a relationship with God.

This brings us back to felicity—God's tranquility personified. The way to find the peaceful life of a rubber band at ease is to be surrendered, relinquished, and resting in the Lord. If we rest totally in Him, we are not stretched. If we relinquish ourselves to Him to do His work, we are at ease. If we are busy praying and praising His majesty, we are at peace because we are where the Lord wants us to be, doing what He created us to do. We are filled with His tranquility.

Certainly we can think we have found happiness and joy while living with sin, but it is a false happiness and joy. With every activity, we are stretched tighter and tighter. Instead, we need to be at rest in God, which brings us real felicity.

Being surrendered to God can be like skiing. In skiing, when I am ready to make a turn, I lower myself and look downhill. My knees go down into the hill, my feet go down an edge, and my whole body drops. This is called anticipation. I simply look down the hill with my whole body dropping and ready. From that point, skiing becomes easy and effortless. I can ski down through the turn with no effort. When that turn is done, I get ready to anticipate the next one and prepare myself for getting through it. I go from one state of anticipation to another, and the skiing is fun and easy.

How do we apply that to our daily lives? When we go through the turns in a state of anticipation with God, believing in His promises, then it is easy to ski through the smooth terrain. When we follow the pull of His gravity, we can negotiate the rough spots better, and we are filled with joy in living with Him.

We have no agenda other than resting in the Lord and listening to Him. We let the Holy Spirit, through faith and prayer, dominate our direction. We do not try to manipulate what happens. We let the Holy Spirit determine our time, our mood, our action. We just say, "Holy Spirit, take over my life and run it. I'm going to flow with you today."

> Do not be anxious about anything, but in everything, by prayer
> and petition, with thanksgiving, present your requests to God.
> And the peace of God, which transcends all understanding, will
> guard your hearts and your minds in Christ Jesus.
> —PHILIPPIANS 4:6–7

There is a lot of talk about burnout in today's world, especially how it affects mothers, fathers, nurses, doctors, teachers, or any caregivers. But when we are relinquished to the Lord, we feel those demands less. By worshiping God's majesty and feeling His joy, we get a turbo boost of power that keeps us going.

There are times when all of us feel that the burden of the world is heavy upon us. There are things about our lives that we cannot control. There is one answer, and that is to be relinquished to the Lord. The peace and joy that we find when we trust in Him are a sure pledge that His joy will be perfected and continue to fill us through all eternity.

Dear Lord, help us to rest in You. Take our burdens and let us enjoy the peace that comes with surrendering our lives to You.

OBEDIENCE

The apostle Paul, writing to the Philippians, describes Jesus as our role model since He is the perfect example of this surrender:

> Your attitude should be the same as that of Christ Jesus: Who, being in very nature God, did not consider equality with God something to be grasped, but made himself nothing, taking the very nature of a servant, being made in human likeness. And being found in appearance as a man, he humbled himself and became obedient to death—even death on a cross!
>
> —PHILIPPIANS 2:5–8

So to relinquish ourselves to God, we must be humble, obedient, and ready to die to our own selfishness. That sounds like a lot. But this is not some dreary task that we do because we have no choice. When we desire God above all other things, we are excited to love Him, believe in Him, obey Him, and serve Him. We get the trust that comes from faith in His grace. "The life I live in the body, I live by faith in the Son of God, who loved me and gave himself for me," Galatians 2:20 says.

Consider the rewards of this joyous mindset. We get the feeling of God in control of our lives. And we get the benefits of following a God who loves us and will provide for us.

> The LORD is my light and my salvation—whom shall I fear? The LORD is the stronghold of my life—of whom shall I be afraid?
>
> — PSALM 27:1

When we are relinquished to God, we are not full of pride or arrogance or selfishness. Remember the fruit of the Spirit—love, joy, peace, patience, kindness, goodness, faithfulness, gentleness, and self-control? These are the qualities that fill us as we surrender ourselves to God and His will. These affect not only our relationship with God but also our relationships with others. Just like that married couple

whose love spills over into all the parts of their lives, so the fruits of a
relinquished life change how we deal with others.

When we are relinquished to God, it is easier to give up the pre-
tenses, pride, and self-righteousness that can destroy relationships
with others. Instead, we respect others with godly dignity. And we
do not need to cover things up. The first couple, Adam and Eve, felt
no need to hide anything from God or each other while they were
relinquished to Him and living without sin. They were open to one
another. They didn't hide their feelings. It was a truly intimate relationship. Only when they sinned did they feel the need to cover themselves with clothes and with selfish attitudes. In the same way, we are
truly intimate with others only when we are relinquished to God and
feel no need to cover up or hide behind false actions and attitudes.

*Father, thank You for love, joy, peace, patience, kindness,
goodness, faithfulness, gentleness, and self control. Help us
to use this fruit in our lives every day.*

CHAPTER 5

THE STRUGGLE TO STAY RELINQUISHED

A LIFE of infinite, glorious joy is a life that is relinquished in faith to God. Think of relinquishing our lives to God as being like a trapeze artist. The trapeze artist must let go of one bar before he can start swinging on the next one. In the same way we must relinquish the bar of the world so we can grab the bar of the Lord. We no longer desire the things of this world; we turn everything over to Him.

And just as a trapeze artist swings from bar to bar, so we struggle with totally relinquishing ourselves to God. It is not a one-time event. It is a process as we build our relationship with God. It is like your relationship with your spouse. That relationship did not happen overnight. There was the time you first met, the time you realized you were in love, the time you truly committed yourself to that person. And even after that commitment, the two of you did not have perfect unity all the time. You have had disagreements and misunderstandings as you have learned to live together. But when harmony and unity are restored, the love is greater; the joy at being back together and still being in love is sweeter. And you have gained a deeper understanding of your spouse.

We are that way with God. We love Him, we commit ourselves to Him, but we still struggle in the relationship. We find it difficult to give up our independence; and sometimes we still think there might be something better out there than what He can provide. We can hinder our ability to surrender ourselves to God.

A LESSON IN TRUST

The Scriptures are filled with examples of people's struggles to stay surrendered to God.

One example in the Old Testament is King Asa. When Asa started his reign, he was a great warrior and religious reformer. He trusted God for great things and had found God to be faithful in doing things beyond what Asa could ask or think.

"LORD, there is no one like you to help the powerless against the mighty. Help us, O LORD our God, for we rely on you, and in your name we have come against this vast army. O LORD, you are our God; do not let man prevail against you," Asa prayed in 2 Chronicles 14:11. And Asa and his troops were victorious in battle.

But then Asa's kingdom was threatened by the king in the north of Israel, Baasha. Rather than trusting God, Asa cut a deal with the king of Syria for help. He forgot that with God nothing shall be impossible. The prophet Hanani rebuked Asa for relying on Syria rather than on the Lord. The king was so angry he put the prophet in chains and continued to turn away from God. What did Hanani tell him?

> For the eyes of the LORD range throughout the earth to strengthen those whose hearts are fully committed to him.
> —2 CHRONICLES 16:9

The king had forgotten how God had provided for him, and he had lost sight of his trust in God. He turned to others rather than God. Hanani wanted him to remember God's love and power.

Asa had forgotten that God delights to show Himself strong on behalf of those whose hearts are set on Him. The verse says "whose hearts are fully committed to him." Other translations say "those whose heart is perfect toward him" or "blameless toward Him." In Hebrew, the verb used is a form of *shalom*, or "those whose hearts are shalomed toward God." *Shalom* in the verb form means completing a vow or fulfilling a covenant. It is used later when Nehemiah rebuilt the walls of Jerusalem. He shalomed them; he finished them.

Let's look at a modern story about someone who had that true shalom. Aniefiok Udo was the son of a Nigerian tribal chief who was killed during the civil war there in the late 1960s. The war set tribe against tribe, group against group, and many people were killed. At this time, Aniefiok was in his early teens. He was so angry and resentful that he was "always fighting with knives on the pretext that [he] wanted to kill someone." Instead, that anger and resentment almost killed him.

Whether his condition was caused by physical, mental, or psychological factors is unknown, but he was near death. And he recognized that his hatred and despair were a big part of his illness. Then he met the Lord. Aniefiok changed from a man of hatred and despair to a man of joy, with a smile that extended from ear to ear. He talks now about how God has reconfirmed His call in his life—to serve Him wherever He sends him.

Aniefiok has earned five different college degrees, finishing at Dallas Theological Seminary, always at the top of his class. He has done well because he changed from a man who totally depended on his anger to one who totally rests in the Lord, surrendering himself and believing in God's eternal promises. The fulfilling of God within his heart has given him peace and joy.

So those whose hearts are perfect toward God are those whose hearts are shalomed toward Him. When we trust not in our own strength, but fix our sights on God's majesty, we have joyous, relinquished hearts that trust and depend on Him and believe in His promises.

Dear God, may our hearts never forget Your promises, and may we be transformed through our surrender to You.

LESSONS IN DAILY LIFE

Just as King Asa was drawn away from a relationship with God, we face temptations today. Often we find ourselves lured by the things and ways of this world. We get diverted in our walk with God, and we lose our joy in Him. Our focus shifts from God to ourselves, and we try to take back what we had once relinquished to Him.

Why does this happen? Sometimes things are going well in our lives and we begin to depend on these happy circumstances. Then we forget to trust in Him and begin to think that we can actually take the credit for the good in our lives.

Or sometimes we get caught up in our troubles. We get so focused on them that they pull us down deeper and deeper, and we forget to seek God. A truly relinquished heart feels true joy in God's presence. But there are times when we feel God is far away. Proverbs 13:12 says, "Hope deferred makes the heart sick, but a longing fulfilled is a tree of life." All of us have had goals or hopes for our lives fall through. But our hearts get sick when we get wrapped up in the disappointment and grief. Then we begin down a path of bitterness, resentment, and self-pity that feeds on our selfishness. We did not get what we wanted, and we sulk about it.

There is no room for God in that mindset. We are not relinquished. We are selfish and want to wallow in our misery. Then the Spirit of God moves within us. We realize the distance between our hearts and Him. We are lonely and frustrated. We see that we cannot rely on ourselves. Then we turn back to God, who is our portion and our all-in-all. And the joy of reuniting with His presence fills us. As the Psalmist wrote:

> You turned my wailing into dancing; you removed my sack-cloth and clothed me with joy…
>
> —PSALM 30:11

Dear Lord, help us every day to examine ourselves and relinquish every part of our lives to You. For in Your loving arms we are filled not with the delights of this world, but with Your joy.

DOING OR BEING?

I have to admit to something. Every day, I am one of the first people to get up, get organized, and start moving vigorously, churning from one task to another. And if I am not careful, all this energy that goes to completing tasks distracts me from letting the Lord fill me with His presence.

I have to remember that everything I do in my tasks and errands and duties is short-lived. The eternal things are unseen—how I believe in God's promises, give Him control of my life, and live in love and humility every day. Then I have the pleasures of God in my heart and the love of God in my works.

The Gospel of Luke tells a story about two sisters with a similar conflict between actions of the hands and attitudes of the heart.

Jesus and His disciples stopped at the home of Mary and Martha to visit and eat. Martha scurried around getting things ready for the meal, and she became agitated because Mary just sat at Jesus' feet, listening to what He said. Martha asked Him, "Lord, don't you care that my sister has left me to do the work by myself? Tell her to help me!" And Jesus replied:

> "Martha, Martha," the Lord answered, "you are worried and upset about many things, but only one thing is needed. Mary has chosen what is better, and it will not be taken away from her."
>
> —LUKE 10:41–42

There are a lot of us out there who are like Martha. We are geared toward getting things done, checking them off "to do" lists, and moving on to some other task. My secretary (who happens to be a preacher's wife) and I are the same way; we are both Marthas. And every morning, Lois and I look at each other and smile. And I say, "Lois, you and I are going to be Marys today." She says, "OK." And she smiles because we are both such Marthas.

But those of us who are Marthas are not hopeless, as long as we remember what is most important: we must surrender ourselves daily in faith to God.

Every year, our family goes skiing at Christmas vacation. I used to read the Bible through during that vacation. That is being a Martha. But it also can be a Mary, if I remember to look into the Lord's eyes as I read. I have to ask, "Did I really look for Christ or was I too busy getting the job done? Was I asking the Lord to fill me with His presence as I read, or was I too busy reading?" We are either asking Him to be within us, or we are blocking Him out.

The first thing I do in the mornings when I get up is bless my wife. She asks me, "Are you being a Mary or Martha in this blessing?" She asks me when I read my Bible during Christmas vacation, "Are you being a Mary or a Martha?" Heather helps me remember to stop and listen to God, to work out a closeness with Him that helps me to relinquish myself daily to Him.

Lord, teach us as Marthas to become more like Mary. Teach us to not try to prove ourselves by tasks and deeds, however good they might be. Teach us to come close to you in meekness. Teach us to be open and honest and show us that nothing matters other than you.

WHAT WE WANT, OR WHAT GOD WANTS?

A heart at peace gives life to the body, but envy rots the bones.
—PROVERBS 14:30

Coveting may be one of the biggest things that keeps us from having a relinquished spirit. The dictionary says coveting is "to long for with envy." For Christians, it means our hearts desire something other than Jesus.

In envy, the Pharisees delivered Christ to be crucified. Good came out of it because Christ was in it. But frequently that envy, or covetousness, is the epitome of sins that separate us from the ability to be relinquished. And if we are not relinquished, we do not have true joy.

In all facets of life we can destroy ourselves by wanting the wrong things or even too much of what we already have. We want when we need not. Our wants keep us from having the joy of relationships that are godly—a godly relationship with each other and a godly relationship with our Redeemer.

People who want a lot of things are frequently anxious about everything and sensitive to everything—their personal lives, their work, their relationships. Some people even destroy their marriages by wanting other things, especially if they become involved in other relationships. Mark 4:19 says, "But the worries of this life, the deceitfulness of wealth and the desires for other things come in and choke the word, making it unfruitful."

I see this inner, destructive motive in my own attitudes; I see it in my relationships with colleagues; I see it in interpersonal relationships. It destroys our productivity, our peace within our work, and everything else in our lives because we are envious of someone else. Instead of being thankful for what we have and feeling grateful and blessed, we feel envious to the point of negating our own place in life and, certainly, our communion with Christ. Envy of worldly things takes away from our surrender to Him because it prevents us from being relinquished. It keeps us in the world rather than focused on the eternal. It keeps us from having faith and joy.

The things we want also keep us from enjoying the things we have. There is an old story about four cows in a field. The field is fenced off into four sections and each cow has her own section to enjoy. Yet each cow has her neck through the fence, trying to get the grass in another cow's section.

Coveting gives us more anxiety and less pleasure. The relinquished life doesn't mean we have "things." When we believe God's promises we are filled with joy, peace, and righteousness. An abandoned faith puts God first, and then we are able to more fully enjoy what He has given us.

The best example is a story Jesus tells in Luke 16:19–26:

> "There was a rich man who was dressed in purple and fine linen and lived in luxury every day. At his gate was laid a beggar named Lazarus, covered with sores and longing to eat what fell from the rich man's table. Even the dogs came and licked his sores.
>
> "The time came when the beggar died and the angels carried him to Abraham's side. The rich man also died and was buried. In hell, where he was in torment, he looked up and saw Abraham far away, with Lazarus by his side. So he called to him, 'Father Abraham, have pity on me and send Lazarus to dip the tip of his finger in water and cool my tongue, because I am in agony in this fire.'
>
> "But Abraham replied, 'Son, remember that in your lifetime you received your good things, while Lazarus received bad things, but now he is comforted here and you are in agony. And besides all this, between us and you a great chasm has been fixed, so that those who want to go from here to you cannot, nor can anyone cross over from there to us.'"

Jesus tells us that there is no correlation between what we have on earth and what we have when we die. Even though Lazarus had nothing and was physically in shame on earth, he had turned his life over to God. And while the rich man had everything, he was proud and arrogant. It kept him from being relinquished. And their positions were reversed when they died. Lazarus is at the right side of Abraham, and the rich man is in torment in hell.

Does this mean that if we have worldly goods we will spend eternity in hell? Not at all. Our possessions do not matter to God. Our attitude toward them does. What we need is abandoned faith and a relinquished spirit. Lazarus had nothing to prevent him from being relinquished; the rich man did. Sometimes we let our possessions or desires keep us from turning to God. Then we struggle with surrendering those things to Him.

We must remember to keep our attitude toward earthly possessions in check. If we begin to believe our possessions make us important, we put our trust in them and become proud and arrogant and depend on our own abilities. But if we remember that everything comes from God, we can keep our focus on Him and live a life that is relinquished to His will. A mighty king of Babylon, Nebuchadnezzar, learned this, and his words still speak to us today.

> Now I, Nebuchadnezzar, praise and exalt and glorify the King of heaven, because everything he does is right and all his ways are just. And those who walk in pride he is able to humble.
> —DANIEL 4:37

Dear God, may our eyes never lose sight of You, that we can focus on eternal treasures and not the possessions of this world.

THE WORRY DISEASE

I would love to be in the stock market. I did some trading when I was young, but it made me worry about what was happening in the world. I was constantly concerned about all the dynamics of the world—the politics, the monetary system, the business cycles, and the ever-intruding Marxist philosophy in various economics.

So I distanced myself, refusing to allow myself to worry. I found that when I would come back to even thinking about it in a very cursory way, just by reading a lot about business and getting involved in planning projects, I removed myself from the peace that I normally had, and I found myself worrying again. And that mentality was certainly not as peaceful or desirable or joyful as the philosophy of simply loving and caring for people in my medical practice.

The lesson I learned was that I had to be relinquished to God. I had to give up worrying about the future and trying to control what would happen to me. I had to forget the worries of the world and believe in God's eternal promises. For us to truly relinquish ourselves to God we have to quit thinking in earthly terms and trust in His agenda and timetable.

> Therefore we do not lose heart. Though outwardly we are wasting away, yet inwardly we are being renewed day by day. For our light and momentary troubles are achieving for us an eternal glory that far outweighs them all. So we fix our eyes not on what is seen, but on what is unseen. For what is seen is temporary, but what is unseen is eternal.
>
> —2 CORINTHIANS 4:16–18

In the medical profession, we see patients who frequently worry themselves sick. They create problems so they have something to worry about. And worry becomes the worst disease I see. It destroys people by destroying the quality of their life, the length of their life—every part of their life. People do this not only with their bodies, but in all facets of their life.

In sporting activities some people worry so much that they destroy their ability to perform at their best. For example, one of the most important things golfers can do is relax and concentrate. But they can worry so much that it affects their game. That is true in any sport. It is very important that we are aware of our elapsed time when running, or our golf score when we are on the course. But we cannot be overcome and let those things make us worry. If we worry too much, we are beaten in a mind game.

We can destroy relationships in the same way. Sometimes two people want to become very close, yet one person is always worrying. That worrying prevents real intimacy because the other person can get only so close without getting caught up in that unhealthy worry mentality. Many husbands and wives have a problem with a spouse who worries too much. It is difficult to have a healthy mental attitude and still be close to their spouse.

What do we do if we have a spouse whose worrying transcends every part of his or her life? Love them, care for them, pray for them, and wait for them to get through that stage so they can blossom. You want them to not worry, so you have to relinquish them to the Lord. By relinquishing them, you also give yourself to the Lord, so you do not get pulled down into that whirlpool of worry. You must be close to your mate, but you must be relinquished at the same time. Anything less and we self-destruct. We must abandon ourselves to God's promises, like John Wesley did at Aldersgate.

Here is something my colleague Gary Carter wrote about worry:

> What are we really saying when we worry?
> We are saying:
> Maybe God doesn't care, after all.
> Maybe God isn't good, after all.
> Maybe God's promises aren't true, after all.
> Maybe God isn't in control, after all.
> Maybe God isn't sovereign, after all.
> Maybe God doesn't work all things for good for those who
>   love Him, after all.
> Maybe God isn't all-wise in the trials He sends us, after all.
> Maybe God isn't a faithful Father, after all.
> What terrible things to say! Let us think about what we are
>   really saying when we worry.

It seems we fall prey to the things we worry about the most. I refuse to worry in my medical practice. I will continue to relinquish myself to the Lord so I can practice the best medicine possible and delight myself in His presence as I try to take care of people.

If I worried about all the facets of my life, life would become just what I worried about. If throughout the day I relinquish myself to Him, to His joy, and to His glorious countenance, I become like Him.

We have the choice to enjoy life or to destroy it with worry and want. When we worry too much, we show that we do not trust the Lord. And when we try to be happy externally and artificially, it fades quickly. We must refuse to worry and want; we have to care only to be relinquished to Him in love. There are many characteristics necessary for any activity—quickness as a tennis player, strength as a football player, submission to the will of God as a Christian. Through submission we will enjoy God's favor.

There is only one answer—relinquishing ourselves to God in absolute faith, faith in His grace that He answers everything. The power of the Resurrection is the answer to all.

> *Dear Lord, keep us strong in our faith in You and Your grace. Help us to put our faith in You when we are more inclined to trust in ourselves. Help us to not be distracted by the trials of daily life, but instead, to rely on Your love and strength.*

A Critical Spirit

Love is essential for us to truly relinquish our lives in faith to God. But sometimes our pride gets the better of us. We can develop a habit of criticizing others to build up ourselves, and we lose sight of that love. We become accusers rather than intercessors. And when that happens, we end up destroying ourselves and the things that are most important to us.

A similar thing happened to Jacob in the Old Testament. Jacob tricked his father, Isaac, into giving him the blessing that rightfully belonged to his older brother, Esau. Then his mother sent him to live with her brother, Laban. While there, Jacob fell in love with Laban's daughter Rachel. He made a deal with Laban. He would work for him for seven years in exchange for Rachel's hand in marriage.

But on the wedding day, Laban tricked Jacob, giving him Rachel's older sister, Leah. So then Jacob had to work another seven years to marry his true love, Rachel.

These two deceitful men lived on the same land until it became unbearable. One night, Jacob gathered up his family and possessions, including all the herds he owned, and left without telling Laban. While the family was packing, Rachel stole her father's household gods, without telling Jacob. Laban was angry that Jacob left and that the household gods were missing, so he chased Jacob.

When Laban found him, he confronted Jacob about the missing gods. He accused Jacob of taking not only his daughters, but his herds and, of course, the household gods. Laban's pride and anger needed to try and put Jacob down one last time.

Jacob defended himself, saying the women and herds were rightfully his. He had worked hard for them. Then he said he did not know anything about the missing gods, and he told Laban to look around. He also issued this curse, which would come back to haunt him, "But if you find anyone who has your gods, he shall not live" (Gen. 31:32).

Now, Jacob did not know that Rachel had hidden her father's possessions in her saddlebag. Without knowing it, he cursed the only thing he truly cared for—his wife Rachel. Laban did not find the missing gods, and he and Jacob parted on bitter terms. What happened to Rachel, whom Jacob unknowingly cursed? She later died in childbirth.

Now, Jacob could have told Laban, "Let me look with you and help you find them." Then the partnership would have grown and there would have been seeds of unity, not disharmony. But he did not, and he lost the one thing he loved most, his wife Rachel.

The lesson for us is to remember to keep a loving and humble spirit. We should use the art of humble questioning rather than being proud and getting critical and angry. Otherwise, we will destroy ourselves and those around us, particularly those who are closest to us.

Lord, help us to follow Your example of love and humility. Keep us from being critical for the sake of our own egos, and help us to act with kindness, not pride.

CHAPTER 6

RELINQUISHED OR RELIGIOUS?

S URRENDER, submission, selflessness. When we make ourselves subservient to God, we find ourselves filled with joy. When we get rid of our egos and independence, we find ourselves filled with glorious, abundant joy. We are at peace with ourselves because we have found peace in God. Then we are full of joy because we love God and depend on Him—not ourselves. However, let us never forget that it is receiving the love of God by believing His promises which is the fountain of our inner life toward God. (See John 4:14.)

Earlier we talked about how the temptations and problems of the world can lure us away from a relinquished life. But some of our fiercest struggles can be as followers of Christ—when we get so busy "doing" all the right things that we forget to be still and listen to Christ and follow him. We do not have peace and joy because we are too busy doing things.

Within all of us there is a tug between the relinquished spirit and a religious one. Now, on the surface, having a religious spirit sounds like a good thing. But by "religious spirit" I mean we are following the religious culture, going through the motions of having faith in God, but not really committing to Him; we do not love Him and we do not truly believe in His promises. We must not just appear externally as if we were religious, by calling ourselves such or belonging to an organization. A relinquished heart changes us from indifference to a life of joy and love that is visible in our actions.

The religious spirit puts man first; the relinquished spirit focuses on God. The relinquished heart finds true joy in God. Joy is missing in a religious spirit. This is a clear concept, but our human nature makes it difficult to accomplish every day.

SUPERFICIAL SIGNS

The Old Testament gives us many examples that illustrate the problems with a religious spirit. Chapter 4 of 1 Samuel tells us about a series of battles between the Israelites and the Philistines. In one battle, the Israelites lost 4,000 men. So they sent the message back to the city of Shiloh: bring the ark of the covenant to the battlefield. The Israelites planned to carry it into the next battle, hoping God would bless them because the ark was present.

The ark contained the tables of the law. But it also had an atonement cover (or mercy seat) to proclaim that there is forgiveness with God. The presence of that cover made it a type of God's throne representing grace. So the ark was not just a physical presence. It was a symbol of God's covenant with His people and their commitment to Him.

There was a precedent for carrying this holy symbol of God into battle. God told Joshua at the battle of Jericho to have priests march at the front of his army carrying the ark. The walls of Jericho collapsed, and Joshua's army was victorious.

But when the Israelites decided to use the ark in their battle against the Philistines, they were not following God's command; they were just looking for an edge in the fight. They wanted the outward blessing of battle—victory—without an inward devotion to God. Bringing the ark to the battle was an outward and showy attempt to manipulate God. This was the religious spirit at its worst—a spirit that relies on false actions, not heartfelt faith. It is not that what they did was just wrong. They did it with the wrong motives.

The Israelites must have been surprised at the outcome. Not only did they lose the battle, but also 30,000 men were killed and the ark was captured by the Philistines. The whole experience was summarized in the word *Ichabod,* which means "the glory has departed," or "the Lord has departed" from Shiloh and all of Israel, with the capture of the ark.

We need to examine our own lives. Do we have God before us or our own goals? Here is one way to look at it:

> I have set the LORD always before me. Because he is at my right hand, I will not be shaken.
>
> —PSALM 16:8

> *Dear God, let us not be shaken, but have our eyes fixed firmly on You. Let our actions speak for our beliefs and let us not have false attitudes and activities that do not reflect Your joy.*

SELFISH SPIRIT

When we have a religious spirit, we are focused more on ourselves and what God can do for us than we are on His majesty and grace and what we can do for Him. We start presenting Him with lists of demands, and we do not want to give Him anything in return. We are selfish and self-centered. We want to do only what is convenient for us. Jesus warns us about this attitude when He quotes the words of the prophet Isaiah as He lectures the Pharisees:

> "These people honor me with their lips, but their hearts are far from me. They worship me in vain; their teachings are but rules taught by men."
>
> —MATTHEW 15:8–9

When we are filled with a religious spirit, our human desire to be independent takes over. We start thinking that we know best. We start relying on our own puny skills and abilities rather than on the limitless power of the Almighty God.

Dr. Martyn Lloyd-Jones, who was born in 1899 in Wales, gave a speech early in his life titled "The Problem with Wales."[1] One of the problems he singled out was with mirrors. He told of how:

> When he grew up in Wales, they didn't have many mirrors. People spent so much time looking in mirrors, it gave them a

conscious focus on self. They were looking at their own face and it was firmly fixed in their mind. They were all the time thinking about their appearance and the impression they made.

Our hearts are not in the right place. We may go through the motions of believing, or follow all the rules, but that does not get us anywhere. Rather than being focused on ourselves we need to follow the advice of the Psalmist:

Look to the LORD and his strength; seek his face always.

—PSALM 105:4

Father, we mean to trust in You and let You have control of our lives. But often we fail. May our joy in You keep us strong.

PRIDE

Humility isn't something that comes naturally to a lot of people. We want to be proud of who we are, what we accomplish, and what we own. There is a kind of true pride, but there is also the false pride of a religious spirit. Here is a warning about false pride:

Do not keep talking so proudly or let your mouth speak such arrogance, for the LORD is a God who knows, and by him deeds are weighed.

—1 SAMUEL 2:3

A relinquished heart requires purity and separation from our base human attitudes, which are constantly within us regardless of how close we are to the Lord. David Jeremiah points out that we frequently think we have the answer. In fact, in our own egotism we think we are "the answer" and frequently do not turn to Christ.

True humility comes with submission to Him and worship of Him. We are not humble by nature. It is not something we decide we can acquire. We become humble only as we love and follow Him. And our submission to Him becomes all-consuming—affecting every part of our body, permeating us, and directing us. Humility becomes ours because we are moldable by the Holy Spirit.

All of you, clothe yourselves with humility toward one another, because, "God opposes the proud but gives grace to the humble." Humble yourselves, therefore, under God's mighty hand, that he may lift you up in due time.

—1 PETER 5:5–6

Dear God, may we keep our own arrogance in check and remember who You are, how much You love us, and how You will continually provide for us.

LEGALISM

When we are filled with a religious spirit, we get wrapped up in following rules and regulations, which is easier than trying to seek God and follow His will. We quit trusting in Him, and we start trying to control our own lives.

Then the Holy Spirit will not work through us. We no longer follow God's major commandment: "Love the LORD your God with all your heart and with all your soul and with all your strength" (Deut. 6:5). Instead, we are filled with a spirit of legalism:

Since you died with Christ to the basic principles of this world, why, as though you still belonged to it, do you submit to its rules: "Do not handle! Do not taste! Do not touch!"? These are all destined to perish with use, because they are based on human commands and teachings.

—COLOSSIANS 2:20–22

Paul warns us how wrong this love of rules and regulations can be:

He has made us competent as ministers of a new covenant—not of the letter [or law] but of the Spirit; for the letter kills, but the Spirit gives life.

—2 CORINTHIANS 3:6

Jesus battled those with a spirit of legalism during His ministry here on earth. He criticized them for following minor rules rather than focusing on loving God.

"Woe to you, teachers of the law and Pharisees, you hypocrites! You give a tenth [as your tithe]…But you have neglected the more important matters of the law—justice, mercy and faithfulness. You should have practiced the latter, without neglecting the former."

—Matthew 23:23

This religious spirit, which was dictated by rules, kept the Jewish leaders from being surrendered to God. They failed to adore and praise God. Jesus preached a relinquished heart that truly believes in God, as the Psalmist wrote:

As the deer pants for streams of water, so my soul pants for you, O God. My soul thirsts for God, for the living God. When can I go and meet with God?

—Psalm 42:1–2

Jesus, help us remember that You are our focus. Let us dwell in You and be Your children for eternity.

Rebellion and Growth

C. S. Lewis would ask intellectuals to imagine, if they could, a God who would provide for them, love them, and be their constant source of strength. Then he would ask whether that would be a bad or good thing. You would think that most intellectuals would say, "Well, that seems good, even though I have a hard time rationalizing God."

Then Lewis would say: Suppose we were created by a person, Elohim the Creator, and that He had a design for us and a love for us, just as a father has for his children. Do you think that would be a good thing?

Of course, the answer has to be "yes." It is a good thing to know that kind of God. But it is difficult for us to accept because of our pride and our rebellion. Our religious spirit when we are self-centered gets in the way. Lewis's writings look at life from eternity's perspective and say that our lives are all a bit of a rebellion against God.

There is another way of looking at it. Each of us develops, to a greater or lesser extent, a passive-aggressive personality as we grow up. It can be defined like this: when your parents told you to sit down, you sat down, but you were still standing up on the inside. That is a form of rebellion. Now, as we grow, we may mature, replacing that rebellion with love for God and others. Then we learn to serve one another and submit to one another.

Or, that rebellion in us can evolve into defiance, which makes us selfish. We insist on always having our own way and are difficult to live with. We can become manipulative, destructive, frustrated, unhappy, and angry.

We develop similarly in our relationship with God. As we struggle to give up our pride and independence and be relinquished to Him, we learn to live in His presence. And that helps us destroy our mental, physical, and sinful rebellion, and we become one with Him.

If we do not mature and learn to submit to Him and serve Him in love, we will never be truly relinquished. An Old Testament story helps us remember this: a man named Nabal, a wealthy man who is described as surly and mean, rejected David's request for some provisions for himself and his men. Not only did he reject the request, but he abused and insulted David. And David, being human, was angered. He told his men to get ready for battle because he intended to destroy Nabal and everything that belonged to him.

Nabal's wife, Abigail, caught wind of what was happening. Without wasting any time, she went to David, bringing an abundance of food and wine, so she could calm him down and save her husband. When she got to David, she asked for his forgiveness, and told him that he would find great satisfaction if wisdom and grace replaced his anger. She spoke with assurance that God would keep him safe, and he need not be troubled by people such as her husband.

> Even though someone is pursuing you to take your life, the life
> of my master will be bound securely in the bundle of the living
> by the LORD your God. But the lives of your enemies he will hurl
> away as from the pocket of a sling.
>
> —1 SAMUEL 25:29

Abigail reminded David that the Lord was his reason for living (his life was bound up in the bundle of life with the Lord) and to put aside his anger. This helped David calm down and gave him a greater perspective. David remembered that he had to surrender to God and seek for Him to be in control.

We must mature in our relationship with God. One way is to remember that Jesus must be our portion in this life—our greatest joy—and that the joy of the Lord is our strength.

> *Dear God, even though we are Your children, we do not want to be childish. Help us grow and mature in our love and help us surrender to You.*

CHAPTER 7

Restored to Joy

I T IS a daily struggle to stay relinquished to God. And sometimes we fail. Our desire for independence and control takes over; we forget God's promises, and we turn away from Him. And our lives can become consumed with bitterness, hatred, frustration, and anger. We are living in sin because we are not living in God's presence.

But God gives us a path back to Him, a way to restore the relationship. When we confess our sin and repent, we experience overwhelming joy in renewing our communion with Him again.

> Create in me a pure heart, O God, and renew a steadfast spirit within me. Do not cast me from your presence or take your Holy Spirit from me. Restore to me the joy of your salvation and grant me a willing spirit, to sustain me.
> —PSALM 51:10–12

In this psalm, David writes of the joy of coming back into a right relationship with God. When we confess our sin and repent, we experience overwhelming joy in knowing Him again. We are filled with wonder and awe at His grace and naturally worship His greatness and majesty. Separation from God means sadness. Reunion with Him means joy and gladness.

Confessing our sin is an important step on the path to a relinquished heart. When we confess, we admit that we have sinned against God's love. Jesus tells a story in Luke 15 to illustrate this. A son asked his father for his inheritance, took the money, and travelled far from home. He squandered all the money, and then he was forced to look for work.

He could only find one job—feeding pigs. He realized his working conditions were worse than those of his father's workers. He decided to go home and ask his father to treat him as he would any other hired hand. "The son said to him, 'Father, I have sinned against heaven and against you. I am no longer worthy to be called your son'" (Luke 15:21).

But the father was not angry that his son had wasted his money and time. He did not take him back as an employee and say, "I told you so," or lecture him. Instead, he rejoiced that his son had come home. He said, "Bring the fattened calf and kill it. Let's have a feast and celebrate. For this son of mine was dead and is alive again; he was lost and is found" (Luke 15:23–24).

Too often we are like that son. We rely on our own abilities and skills, and we do not trust in the Lord with all our hearts. We are ungrateful when we receive blessings from God, and we do not give Him the credit. And we do not admit that we are living in this sinful attitude. Our actions speak louder than our false words. They show that we do not believe God is worthy of our loyalty. We have turned from a relinquished spirit to a false pride and trust in our own strength and understanding.

As the prodigal son confessed his unworthiness, so we must admit that we have dishonored God. We do not confess because we were caught at our sin or were embarrassed by it. We must confess because we have offended the God who loves us. As Proverbs 28:13 says, "He who conceals his sins does not prosper, but whoever confesses and renounces them finds mercy." We must be honest, we must be specific, and we must be thorough when we confess our sins to God.

> *Father, I am such a rebellious child. Lord, my motives were from love of myself, not love and praise of You.*

SEEKING GOD'S FORGIVENESS

After we have confessed our sins, we must ask God's forgiveness: "Oh, pity and forgive me by the blood of Christ." When we ask His forgiveness, we surrender ourselves to Him and are cleansed. Then nothing stands between our Redeemer and us.

Then we must rise up and praise Him for forgiveness. We believe it. We embrace it. We delight in it. "I'm forgiven! I'm clean before the Lord!" After all, God has promised He would forgive us. It is His desire for us to ask. First John 1:9 says, "If we confess our sins, he is faithful and just and will forgive us our sins and purify us from all unrighteousness." Second Chronicles 7:14 says, "If my people, who are called by my name, will humble themselves and pray and seek my face and turn from their wicked ways, then will I hear from heaven and will forgive their sin and will heal their land." We treat God as a liar if we do not truly believe we are forgiven and rejoice.

Then we have the joy of being free from sin. Until we seek His forgiveness, we cannot have that kind of joy. That forgiveness, that freedom is essential.

Because we are human, we all seem to wander right back into things that we should not do; we deviate from His standard. So asking forgiveness is not just a one-time event. We need to constantly be aware of our thoughts, our actions, our lack of action, and anything else in which we fail. Paul describes this state of sinful living in Romans 14:23: "Everything that does not come from faith is sin." Let us not be of anything other than faith in Him. We should have no agenda other than seeking to please Him, to fellowship with Him, to serve Him, and to seek forgiveness when we sin.

Dear Lord, forgive us when we stray from You and lose sight of Your glory, majesty, and love. And we praise You for Your mercy, grace, and forgiveness, which frees us from our sinful lives.

REPENTANCE

If you repent, I will restore you.

—JEREMIAH 15:19

When we confess our sins and seek God's forgiveness, we realize who we are and how majestic God is. We see the awesome power of His grace, that He would continue to love us and want a relationship with us even though we sin against Him. It is a state of repentance that overwhelms us. There is a sweet brokenness that accompanies the tears of remorse, the melting and relenting of the soul returning to God, lamenting its former unkindness. "A broken and contrite heart, O God, you will not despise," Psalm 51:17 says. Repentance is a delightful experience that flows from love. Our love for God is met with His love for us because we are relinquished to Him and believe in Him. In that relationship we lose ourselves to the one we love, namely God, and care about ourselves only because He cares for us.

We cannot be relinquished if our hearts are filled with anger or bitterness or if we are not willing to forgive others. The relinquished heart does not allow those attitudes. And those attitudes do not permit relinquishment. To be relinquished, to find the joy that comes from seeking God's presence, we must give up the selfishness that feeds anger and bitterness. We must forgive others as God forgives us.

We need to believe the words of promise about repenting of our sin and turning our hearts to God.

> Repent, then, and turn to God, so that your sins may be wiped out, that times of refreshing may come from the Lord.
>
> —ACTS 3:19

But Jesus does not just forgive us. He is as determined to make us holy as He is to forgive us. Titus 2:14 says He "gave himself for us to redeem us from all wickedness and to purify for himself a people that are his very own, eager to do what is good." This was His intention on the cross. He was not only saying, "Father, redeem them, forgive them, pardon them." He was equally saying, "Father make them holy, purify them, and bring them to a surrendered and relinquished heart."

> *Father, take our sins, burdens, and our selfishness and forgive us. Help us to live pure and sinless lives that worship You and enjoy Your peace and joy.*

CHAPTER 8

WORSHIP AND JOY

Blessed are those who have learned to acclaim you, who walk in the light of your presence, O LORD. They rejoice in your name all day long; they exult in your righteousness.

—PSALM 89:15–16

HAVE you ever almost worshiped someone, such as a teacher when you were in second grade, the homecoming king or queen, or maybe even a movie star or singer? It is an overwhelming, uncontrollable devotion, even a passion. We would give up everything for that person, and we would do everything in our power to be just like him or her.

Now compare that with worshiping God. It is a much greater relationship than anything we experience with another human being because when we believe in God, we begin to see His power and glory and grace. We behold His countenance, and we are overwhelmed by His majesty. Worship should be our only response to God, the Beginning and the End, the Maker of heaven and earth, our Creator and Redeemer.

Many, O LORD my God, are the wonders you have done. The things you planned for us no one can recount to you; were I to speak and tell of them, they would be too many to declare.

—PSALM 40:5

All things are of God, all things are through God, all things are sustained by the breadth of His might. His knowledge is without bounds. His wisdom is infinite. His riches are immense and inexhaustible. His majesty is awe-inspiring. His omnipotent power is seen from the galaxies to the mysteries of a single cell.

> The heavens declare the glory of God; the skies proclaim the work of his hands.
>
> —PSALM 19:1

In Him we live and move and have our being. We open our eyes and know He is there. He has rained down blessings from heaven upon the earth where He has placed us. This rich and well-furnished world provides all our necessities. And while we are busy spinning in the direction of one year, He is preparing for another.

God is infinitely above any need that we may have of Him. He is above our reach. He is above our conceptions; we cannot comprehend Him. Yet when we surrender our lives to God and believe in His promises, we find our ultimate existence and purpose in Him.

Once we are in God's presence, we cannot help but worship His majesty and praise Him. We also cannot help but find joy in God's grace and power. There is no other way to feel when we fall at the feet of the Master. We are in awe of the salvation and fellowship He offers.

Compare this with the beliefs of a group of Epicurean and Stoic philosophers the apostle Paul met in Athens. Epicureans believed it was hopeless to search by reason for pure truth, so they sought true pleasure through experience. Stoics believed in human self-sufficiency and stern self-repression.

They were intrigued by what Paul had to say about Christianity. His words still speak to us today:

> The God who made the world and everything in it is the Lord of heaven and earth and does not live in temples built by hands. And he is not served by human hands, as if he needed anything, because he himself gives all men life and breath and everything else. From one man he made every nation of men, that they should inhabit the whole earth; and he determined the times

set for them and the exact places where they should live. God
did this so that men would seek him and perhaps reach out for
him and find him, though he is not far from each one of us. 'For
in him we live and move and have our being.' As some of your
own poets have said, 'We are his offspring.'

—ACTS 17:24–28

Indeed, the excellency of His nature creates the fires of worship,
the desire to praise and glorify Him. Worship is not an end toward
something; it is an end in itself. The goal of worship is not to see what
we can get out of it; the goal of worship is to exalt God. Worship is
gladly reflecting to God the radiance of His worth; it is a spontaneous
emotion that genuinely comes from the heart.

Father, you are Lord and You are God. Let us fall at Your
feet and worship You as our Maker, Redeemer and Savior.

LOVE AND WORSHIP

Whatever we love, we praise. Whatever we love, we delight in, and
we enjoy. But this love, this enjoyment, this delight, is incomplete
until we can express it. And we express our love and delight to God
by worshiping Him. He wants us to adore and worship and exalt
Him. When we do that, we cannot help but be filled with joy. "I will
praise you, O LORD, with all my heart; I will tell of all your wonders,"
Psalm 9:1 says.

John Piper, in his book, *Desiring God*, calls this joy and pleasure in
God, "Christian hedonism."[1] We are satisfied with the excellency of
God. We are overwhelmed with the joy of His fellowship. This is the
feast of Christian hedonism, full of spiritual, godly pleasures.

This hedonistic approach is the only humble approach because
it comes with empty hands, depending totally upon God for our
pleasures and acknowledging that He alone can satisfy the heart's
longing to be happy. We love God and are filled with joy at being in
His presence.

Jonathan Edwards said religious affections and charity, or love, are
the fountain of true religion in the heart.[2] Anything other than that is
false, and without this affection and feeling, religion is dead. We worship God because we love Him and believe His promises.

I start each of my prayers by saying, "Lord, we love you." I want to bring out the fact that religion is an affection. Edwards said, "True religion, in most part, consists of heavenly affections and sensible exercisings of the inclination and will of the soul."[3]

> Then will I go to the altar of God, to God, my joy and my delight. I will praise you with the harp, O God, my God.
> —PSALM 43:4

If we love someone, we treat that person with appreciation, attention, tenderness, and honor. Husbands and wives must love and appreciate each other and care for each other; otherwise, they can get critical, selfish, negative, and judgmental. We must be appreciative in any relationship: with a friend, a coworker, a business partner, or neighbors. It is essential for us to appreciate each other; otherwise, we cannot encourage, praise, intercede for, or love others.

Just as we know in our relationships with others who really care for us, God knows how much we love and appreciate Him. Our worship of Him parallels how thankful we are for His grace, majesty, glory, sovereignty, and perfect will. From that love and thanksgiving come a constant state of joy, worship, and prayer that permeates us. First Thessalonians 5:16–18 describes this constant state of being:

> Be joyful always; pray continually; give thanks in all circumstances, for this is God's will for you in Christ Jesus.

The times when I am truly able to let all earthly concerns go, I find myself in a "thanksgiving frenzy." It is a time in my relationship with God when I am so filled with joy in His presence that I thank Him for everything I can think of; I am in a state of total abandonment to my faith in Him. I can gauge how close I am to Him and how far away I have turned from my own personal needs. I am no longer really within myself; I am lifted up into His presence.

I feel closer to God than I do at other times. I just thank Him, knowing my lack and His greatness. He is from the beginning of time and all through eternity, and yet He is at the center of my little life. These thanksgiving frenzies allow me to worship Him in a special way—I do not have to carry a tune or be a great theologian. I simply appreciate the Lord God Almighty, who is everything to me.

Now, I cannot experience these thanksgiving frenzies all the time. But I do seek to be constantly in a state of faith, joy, and worship. For example, as I see patients I say, "We're thankful and blessed for the outcome." That reminds me to be focused on the Lord and thankful to Him for whatever happens. I can use various ways to stay focused: simply by saying Bible verses or praying. It is a constant flow of attention to God.

But all of us should seek this attitude of faith, joy, and worship. We must make it part of all our life and realize it is the only important thing that we are doing at any time. Whether we are practicing our chosen profession, participating in the activities of our daily lives, or simply kneeling in prayer with no one watching, we need to be focused on God. What counts is that feeling of satisfaction we get from exalting Him. This background of love and worship that meditates on His goodness and His love is essential to a peaceful, abundant, godly, and joyous life!

Lord, we stand in awe of Your majesty, Your grace, Your love.
May we always honor You with all our thoughts, desires,
and actions and always believe Your promises.

EXALTING AND BEING EXALTED

More than anything the Lord wants from us, He wants us to praise and worship Him and only Him, unconditionally and without reservations. He tells us this in the Old Testament. Speaking to Moses in Exodus 34:14, God said, "Do not worship any other god, for the LORD, whose name is Jealous, is a jealous God."

God said He would tolerate no rivals for the loyalty of the people of Israel. His name, or character, is "Jealous." In the same way, He demands that same kind of exclusive devotion from us. God wants what is rightfully His. How should we respond? Praise should be given to God for who He is, so we lift Him up, or exalt Him.

It may seem strange that a God who is supposed to be all-loving wants to be all-exalted. But it is not a vain desire; He wants our worship because He gives Himself back to us when we worship Him. He asks us to exalt Him with everything we have, and with our exaltation we are lifted up.

God wants us to be part of His glory, to come under the cloak of His exaltation so we are lifted up and feel the presence of God. Now, it might seem selfish to us that God wants our total devotion, worship, and faith. Yet that is exactly the way it is. It is simply the affirmation of the Creator for the created, and the created for the Creator.

> Yours, O LORD, is the greatness and the power and the glory and the majesty and the splendor, for everything in heaven and earth is yours. Yours, O LORD, is the kingdom; you are exalted as head over all.
>
> —1 CHRONICLES 29:11

Jesus told us the greatest commandments are to "Love the Lord your God with all your heart and with all your soul and with all your mind" and "Love your neighbor as yourself" (Matthew 22:37, 39). And while in worldly realms it may appear selfish, in godly terms it is the epitome of unselfishness. Maybe we should call it godly selfishness. In godly selfishness we realize the best thing we can do is worship God and give worth to others. This godly selfishness benefits us, and it benefits others. What we gain is a closer relationship with God, which helps everyone.

Human, or carnal, selfishness is something we maintain solely for ourselves. Godly selfishness is the only way to ascribe worth to God and to others. So, worship is a self-advantageous thing: it not only lifts us up, but it lifts up all the relationships around us.

We can see this in the way we deal with people every day. If we attempt to encourage people by loving them, caring for them, and seeing the good in them—rather than looking down on them—we are blessed ourselves. A person who spends all day at work trying to be indifferent to people, in effect putting them down, will become that way with a spouse.

On the other hand, a person who ascribes worth to coworkers, looking for their best and attempting to pick them up, carries over that attitude to the home and relationships with family and friends.

If we can take our selfishness away from ourselves and make it godly, our whole life is changed. Rather than looking into the carnal parts of our lives, we look into the divine parts, developing godly dignity.

Our highest good and joy come from keeping our focus on God. True worship is personal, real, and deeply satisfying. Our self enters into the greatest experience of our existence when we worship God.

In any relationship in which two people care about each other, each strives to make the other happier. That is true as we worship God. We want to make Him happier and exalt him. And as He is exalted, He cares to make us happy by giving us a closer relationship with Him.

I once knew a little girl named Felicity. I thought she was beautiful. I am sure when she grew up many men who saw her thought, "My, she would provide a great deal of joy and peace," which is what the word felicity suggests.

However, no person can do that for another. It is empty striving to think we can obtain that felicity, that joy and peace, in anything other than our exaltation of God. With our exaltation we accept a pearl of His exaltation, which is the greatest gift we can receive. That pearl of His presence gives us the fruit of the Spirit—love, joy, peace, patience, kindness, goodness, faithfulness, humility, and self-control—that come from simply praising Him.

Jonathan Edwards sums it up this way in his sermon, "The Unique Excellency of Christ": "In the person of Christ we meet infinite glory and lowest humility. In no other person, do we find this paradox truly perfected. It is His divine nature: the infinitely adorable, and yet with no pride. Christ has the deepest reverence toward God and equality with God. He has infinite worthiness of good and the greatest patience under the suffering of evil. He has exceeding obedience and yet supreme domination over heaven and earth. In Christ is brought together absolute sovereignty and perfect resignation. In Him we see self-sufficiency and an entire trust in God. He has infinite majesty and yet utter humility, to be our servant."[4]

> *Lord God, as we worship You, change us. Fill us with true humility and love that we may better love You and serve those around us.*

DUTY OR LOVE?

You crowned him with glory and honor.

—HEBREWS 2:7

Throughout the Bible we are told that we should crown the Lord with glory and honor. He wants honor and splendor to be given to Him, but given freely and voluntarily. C. S. Lewis once described it as a Christian duty for everyone to be as happy as he can. Joy strengthens us in our service and in our work for God.

Let me explain with an example. I come home on my wedding anniversary with a dozen red roses for my wife and she says, "My, you have these beautiful roses for me. Why did you do it?" Suppose I reply, "I did it because it is my duty. A man should have character and should give his wife roses for their anniversary." Such a response would not go over well. It would not make her heart glad. Nor does it make the Lord glad if we do everything merely out of duty.

Suppose I tell my wife, "Heather, I just want to be with you; I just want to hold your hands and be close to you. These red roses are just a token of how my heart feels—wanting to be as close as possible to you. Let's spend the day together." She would respond very differently to my expression of love than to one of duty. It is not my duty so much that pleases her, it is my joy, my honor, to be with her.

The Lord also wants our love rather than just our sense of duty. We need to delight in Him and He will give us the request of our heart—namely the satisfaction and joy of the Holy Spirit.

Not long ago Chuck Colson was one of the speakers at a meeting.[5] Chuck is a fabulous Christian and one of the greatest citizens of America today. He expounds the gospel of Jesus Christ in a very courageous way and he is faithful, fervent, and focused.

At this meeting, Chuck gave his usual talk about the duty of Christianity. He is a good lawyer, and he analyzed everything very well, discussing duty to God and country, duty to society, duty to our families, and many other duties we as Christians need to recognize. He used many Scripture references, including Ephesians 2:10, which is right after the verse stressing that we are saved by grace. "For we are God's workmanship, created in Christ Jesus to do good works, which God prepared in advance for us to do." Chuck Colson is right! We have duties to do in the church.

Immediately after Chuck's talk, a theologian with a much more demure presentation said, "I don't want to disagree with you, Mr. Colson, but I think it's much more important for us to have the joy of the Lord in our heart than for us to be involved in tasks. It's more important that we be filled with God's Spirit."

The speaker was John Piper, whose books include *The Pleasures of God* and *Desiring God*. In his books he points out the need for the joy of the Lord within our hearts so we enjoy God and God enjoys us.[6] It is easy for us to justify ourselves by our actions, our tasks: giving money, going to the mission field, "doing" in the name of the Lord. But we really cannot have the joy of the Lord in our hearts until we surrender to Him, confess our sins, and ask for forgiveness, making our lives clean.

Many of Piper's thoughts are based on the book *The Life of God in the Soul of Man* by the Reverend Henry Scougal, first published in the 1700s.[7] George Whitefield, an eighteenth century evangelist, said he had finally understood "true religion" is the union of the soul with God, and Christ formed within is, after he had read that treatise.[8]

Scougal points out that we really cannot ever have God's true joy until we have eliminated desire for the things of the world and have released all our resentments. We cannot have the joy of God until we have surrendered all to Him. We can do all the works in the world, but unless we have His anointing, they do not mean anything.

The Westminster Catechism sums it up this way:[9]

> The chief end of man is to glorify God and enjoy Him forever.

When I first read that statement years ago it seemed like very light reading and simplistic theology. It seemed almost too easy to do. But I have come to understand that God does not want just words of praise. He wants us to commit our lives to worshiping Him with a relinquished heart—one that genuinely feels His presence in our lives.

> Therefore, I urge you, brothers, in view of God's mercy, to offer your bodies as living sacrifices, holy and pleasing to God—this is your spiritual act of worship.
>
> —ROMANS 12:1

When our hearts are relinquished to Him, we hand over control of our lives; we become living sacrifices. This relinquished life is the way we worship Him. And when we praise and worship Him with a relinquished heart, we find true freedom and joy because we no longer have to do anything more than worship His majesty as His creation.

As Paul writes:

> So that Christ may dwell in your hearts through faith. And I pray that you, being rooted and established in love, may have power, together with all the saints, to grasp how wide and long and high and deep is the love of Christ, and to know this love that surpasses knowledge—that you may be filled to the measure of all the fullness of God.
>
> —EPHESIANS 3:17–19

It is that simple. Exalt, or worship, God. Enjoy Him. Be filled with joy.

I think our tasks are good, but they must be balanced with religious affections. That balance comes with maturity as a Christian; our "ought to's" become our "want to's." It is just as Jesus said:

> I have food to eat that you know nothing about.…to do the will of him who sent me and to finish his work.
>
> —JOHN 4:32, 34

Dear Lord, help us to submit to You in love. Help us relinquish our hearts and minds and souls to You in the charity that You have given us. And thank You for the joy and felicity that fill our lives of abandonment to Your promises.

WORSHIP CHANGES US

Praise, love, and enjoyment of God produce in us an everlasting felicity and bliss as we struggle in a world that is mean and contemptible, that can destroy everything we are and own. All of us have found ourselves encumbered by our worldly lusts. Yet felicity requires purity and separation from those attitudes, which are constantly with us regardless of our relationship with the Lord.

As we think of God and praise and worship Him, we realize how far short of Him we fall. We grow humble and have the lowest thoughts of ourselves. This is true humility because it results from worshiping God with everything we have and relinquishing ourselves to Him. It is not something we decide to acquire. It comes from worshiping Him. As our worship becomes all-consuming, affecting every part of our person, humility becomes ours because we are moldable by His Holy Spirit that overflows to us. That humility is essential for the happiness and bliss that come with godly felicity.

So by desiring true worship, with faith in His promises, above everything else—works, tithing, duties—everything comes into balance. We end up tithing, we end up doing works, we end up "being" before "doing." In our striving to exalt Him, we begin to walk after Him and become more like Him.

> And we, who with unveiled faces all reflect the Lord's glory, are being transformed into his likeness with ever-increasing glory, which comes from the Lord, who is the Spirit.
>
> —2 Corinthians 3:18

When we look in an everyday mirror, we see a reflection of ourselves. But this verse tells us of another image. Paul writes of the Word of God as a mirror, reflecting to us the Lord Jesus Christ and His glory. We stand in awe and wonder at such a Person, such a Savior, as our Lord Jesus. We behold His glory and want to worship His majesty.

> You have made known to me the path of life; you will fill me with joy in your presence, with eternal pleasures at your right hand.
>
> —Psalm 16:11

David tells us that we have a fullness of joy in God's presence, joy that comes when we behold God's countenance, when we are caught up in His majesty, when we relinquish ourselves. Being in His presence has to change us because it is so overwhelming.

When we worship His majesty, the Holy Spirit changes us. We are changed into His image, from glory to glory. We relinquish self and worship His majesty. Our job is simply to adore Him and worship Him. Our greatest desire is that our Maker is pleased. God is infinitely happy in Himself, and nothing is going to shake or unsettle His throne.

In turning back to God, we cannot take things personally and internalize them. By internalizing, we change our biology, our physiology, and our outlook. We change the way we think and what we become. Instead, we must truly look to the Lord with a relinquished heart and mind.

One of my friends used to tell me that he needed to pray earnestly a minimum of forty-five minutes each morning. His prayers did not make him perfect, but they brought him closer to God. He had more problems and sins than anybody else would admit, but he was honest enough to admit his failures.

Like him, I have every distraction in the world. And like him, prayer brings me back when I totally abandon myself and exalt the Lord. That abandonment, similar to the abandonment seen in physical love, brings us to a deeper relationship with God, and a more beautiful tranquility and felicity permeate our whole being. We have an afterglow of peace that is overwhelming. When a person comes together with God in worship, he personifies a tranquility that is associated with knowing God, being close to God, worshiping Him in ecstasy, and then having a nature that is totally changed because of His closeness. We become what we pray, and our prayers become us.

The fire of devotion and adoration is always kept alive by our attitude when we are active in other things. We should be in such a state of worship that life does not become an effort. It becomes a matter of believing in His promises and relaxing in His felicity. Then our lives are transformed from effort and duty to a state of meditation on the glory of God and willing service from the heart.

The diamonds of God's majesty are needed to plow up a heart as hard as mine. Only then can I receive the seeds that are His precious Word. Only when His majesty truly touches my heart can his Word fill my whole being. Then these seeds will flourish and grow because I believe fully in His promises and respond to Him in worship. No longer do I live with worry or want. I surrender my concerns and desires to Him, and I live a life full of belief and worship. The jewels of His crown enter my eyes, and I see as He sees. Then He has truly changed me. I see the glory of God in everything and relinquish it all to Him.

> But may all who seek you rejoice and be glad in you; may those
> who love your salvation always say, "The LORD be exalted!"
>
> —PSALM 40:16

Chapter 9

A Joyous Life

J oy is the natural outpouring of our hearts as God's presence becomes the central pillar of our lives. Psalm 16:11 says, "You will fill me with joy in your presence." How wonderful that sounds. When we choose God to be the focus of our hearts, we are transformed. We do not look at ourselves and our lives in the same way. We do not worry about events, we do not long for the things of this world, we do not try to find happiness in other people or in our work or play. When we turn ourselves over to God, we cannot help but be joyful, for God is our joy.

Author C. S. Lewis writes about this transformation in his autobiography.[1] He says that from childhood he found that he was always longing for something, and he believed that "something" was joy. After his conversion, as he writes at the end of his autobiography, he asks, "What about my search for joy?" His answer: "After I found God, I didn't think much more about it."

Joy is not the product of seeking after joy; it is the product of seeking after Jesus. It is the feeling that comes from being centered on Him and not on ourselves. As C. S. Lewis points out, joy is a response to the presence of God's love in our souls. People who seek after true godly joy don't look to themselves; they look to God.

There is a story about a memory expert who appeared on an interview show. The expert kept calling the interviewer Bob when his real name was Bill. The interviewer tried correcting the guy a couple of times, but he kept calling the interviewer Bob.

This person, who is supposed to understand how memory works, is like many of us, who are supposed to understand the relinquished heart and the joy of relinquished worship. We do not show that joy, we do not show that relinquishment. So we are very much like that memory expert who cannot remember names. We cannot remember to be relinquished and have faith in God's grace. And then our lives do not show the things they should—the fruit and gifts of the Spirit.

Everything in the Bible points out that we must first have a true desire for, and a genuine affection toward, God. When we are focused on appearances, we have a religious spirit. When it comes from within, when our hearts are surrendered completely to God's will, we are filled with joy and felicity.

Dear Lord, may faith in You fill us with Your fruit and Your felicity.

JOY AND LAUGHTER

Holy joy is not us trying to build up something within ourselves. It is having a true inner joy. And that joy bubbles out of us in genuine love and laughter.

I once had the opportunity to fish in Alaska with Chuck Swindoll. When we were there, one thing I did in addition to fish was listen to Chuck. And I do not remember a half-hour going by in which Chuck was not laughing. He really laughs! I have never met a person who laughs as much as Chuck Swindoll. And it is genuine—he is enjoying himself. He has holy joy! He lives Philippians 4:4: "Rejoice in the Lord always. I will say it again: Rejoice!"

All of us should have the joy of God explode within us. We should burst out with joy and laughter.

The son of Abraham and Sarah was named Isaac, which means "laughter" or "he laughs." As an adult, Isaac reopened wells that had been dug in the time of Abraham, which the Philistines had stopped up after Abraham had died. Isaac freed up the wells so the water could flow.

In the same way, laughter is important as a way of freeing ourselves up. Frequently we become so serious or so burdened by responsibility that we destroy our ability to laugh, and this damages our ability to be in fellowship with God.

But we should be tuned in to the person of Jesus, full of the spontaneity of emotion, of laughter, of love, and of caring. Isaac opened up the wells that had been clogged up by the enemy. Those opened wells gave freedom to his people. In the same way, laughter opens us up from the resentment, anger, hate, and bitterness that destroy the spirit. It releases all the stress and anxiety in us and frees us.

Dear God, may our laughter and love come genuinely from You. May our hearts be filled with the joy that comes from believing in You.

EXPLOSIONS OF JOY

Finally, brothers, whatever is true, whatever is noble, whatever is right, whatever is pure, whatever is lovely, whatever is admirable—if anything is excellent or praiseworthy—think about such things. Whatever you have learned or received or heard from me, or seen in me—put it into practice. And the God of peace will be with you.

—PHILIPPIANS 4:8–9

Paul tells us first to think and then to act. Christianity is not just some theory in our heads; it is in our hearts and in our lives. When we truly believe and act out the obedience and direction the Lord calls us to, it is a total experience. The felicity of God will explode within us.

Many people have had, or pursued, deeper experiences with God. These may be physical manifestations of the joy that comes from being in God's presence. Ultimately, we should evaluate these experiences according to the Word of God. But there can be no doubt that some have truly been touched by God's presence.

Many people throughout church history have been filled with experiences of joy. For example, John Wesley and his friend George Whitefield had been having a rough time working for the Lord. So on New Year's Eve, 1738, they bowed in prayer for twelve hours straight. In this time of prayer they were completely abandoned to the Lord. They turned everything over to Him. Then, about 3 a.m., New Year's Day, a great joy came over both of them. They started singing and burst forth in a joy that was almost beyond expression. They were really afraid to tell other people, for fear others would think they were insane.

Then there was Sarah Edwards, Jonathan Edwards' wife. She went through a period of spiritual dryness. Then she went into a very deep time of prayer, and she got what we could describe as "maximum godliness." She developed an enthusiasm and a joy that caused people to almost think she was insane. People said she had "distemper and distortion." Jonathan Edwards replied, "If she has distemper, I'd like to have a little of that distemper. And if she's distorted, the whole church should be distorted."[2] He was very proud that she had exemplified a deeper walk and great godly affection. He thought many who had greater learning and understanding of theology did not feel some of the affections his wife felt. The understanding without the affection is sterile.

Sarah Edwards felt it was important to keep these experiences in perspective. She described a man who came by to talk about the revival. "Just then Mr. W. came in and with a somewhat light, smiling air spoke of the flourishing state of religion in the town." She could scarcely bear to see him speak in this manner. She thought he was too frivolous. She writes, "It seemed to me that we ought to greatly revere the presence of God and to behave ourselves with the utmost solemnity and humility when so great and holy a God was so markedly present and to rejoice before Him with trembling."[3]

All of us should pursue deep experiences with God, but there is an appropriate manner in which to do so.

Sarah Edwards's words about her own experiences guide us in this:

> My mind was so deeply impressed with the love of Christ and a sense of his immediate presence, that I could with difficulty refrain from rising from my seat and leaping for joy. I continued to enjoy this intense and lively refreshing sense of divine

things, accompanied with strong emotions, for nearly an hour.
After which I experienced a delightful calm and peace and rest
in God until I retired for the night. And during the night, both
waking and sleeping, I had joyful views of divine things and a
complacent rest of the soul of God.[4]

When we are relinquished to God and feel privileged to be one
with Him, that privilege engenders an appreciation that manifests
a joy within our hearts. When our laughter is motivated by Christ
Himself, we know we have the true balance in heavenly joy.

Father, we earnestly seek Your presence in our daily lives.
Fill us with the tranquility that comes from believing in
Your promises.

CARING FOR OTHERS

When we are filled with joy, we cannot keep it shut up inside us. It
has to come out and fill all the parts of our lives and overflow into
our relationships with others. We cannot be joyful on the inside, yet
cranky on the outside. It will not work. Jesus explains it this way:

You are the light of the world. A city on a hill cannot be hidden.
Neither do people light a lamp and put it under a bowl. Instead
they put it on its stand, and it gives light to everyone in the house.
In the same way, let your light shine before men, that they may
see your good deeds and praise your Father in heaven.
—MATTHEW 5:14–16

We cannot keep to ourselves the love and joy that fill us when we
are in communion with God. It pours out of us and onto others. And
we are excited to love him and serve them. Everything that would
benefit others makes us rejoice, and we share all of their happiness.

We are no longer filled with self-importance: "If anyone thinks he
is something when he is nothing, he deceives himself," Galatians 6:3
warns. Instead, we follow the words of Paul and, with a relinquished
heart, put others first:

Do nothing out of selfish ambition or vain conceit, but in
humility consider others better than yourselves. Each of you

should look not only to your own interests, but also to the interests of others.

—PHILIPPIANS 2:3-4

We also find great joy in serving. Psalm 100:2 says to serve the Lord with gladness. The Scottish Metrical Psalms say to serve Him "with mirth." How much easier and more pleasant service is if we do it with mirth and gladness. It is our pleasure, not merely our obligation. And that joy gives us the strength for service—to do the job right.

Remember Mary and Martha? While Mary enjoyed sitting in Jesus' presence, Martha was busy scurrying around getting a meal ready. When we are filled with joy, we are no longer like Martha. We become like Mary in our hearts, focused on Jesus. We can still work hard, but our tasks are done joyfully, out of the desire to do well, not just the need to have things done.

In whatever you do, we need to realize that we are aligning ourselves to God and not just trying to work in our own strength. We are working out a closeness with God.

As we praise God and receive joy and felicity from that praise, we are caught up in glorifying Him, and we become full of charity and obedience. We may be partakers in all the happiness of other people, their inward endowments, and their outward prosperity.

Lord, let us find our peace, joy, and rest centered in Calvary.
May that peace and joy always be within our hearts.

CHAPTER 10

JOY AND PEACE

A BRAHAM was an old man when his son Isaac was born. God had promised that Abraham would be the father of a great nation. And after a great trial of waiting, along came Isaac. Then after a few years, God told Abraham to offer Isaac as a burnt offering. Can you imagine? Abraham was being asked to kill his son, his promise of all the future. But Abraham trusted God. He took Isaac, a knife, and some wood and went up Mount Moriah, exactly as God had told him.

Notice his response. Abraham did not question God; he submitted to God's request and promptly did as God asked. He did not ask others for advice. We do not even know if he asked his wife, Sarah, Isaac's mother. He worked out all the details of the trip and set out. And even though it took three days to reach the place to which God directed him, Abraham still did not doubt God. In faith, he kept on going, knowing God would provide.

> When they reached the place God had told him about, Abraham built an altar there and arranged the wood on it. He bound his son Isaac and laid him on the altar, on top of the wood. Then he

75

reached out his hand and took the knife to slay his son. But the angel of the LORD called out to him from heaven, "Abraham! Abraham!" "Here I am," he replied. "Do not lay a hand on the boy," he said. "Do not do anything to him. Now I know that you fear God, because you have not withheld from me your son, your only son."

—GENESIS 22:9–12

Abraham was totally abandoned in faith to God. He was totally surrendered to His will. He was willing to do whatever God asked, knowing God would provide the answer.

By faith Abraham, when God tested him, offered Isaac as a sacrifice. He who had received the promises was about to sacrifice his one and only son, even though God had said to him, "It is through Isaac that your offspring will be reckoned." Abraham reasoned that God could raise the dead, and figuratively speaking, he did receive Isaac back from death.

—HEBREWS 11:17–19

In one of his sermons, C. H. Spurgeon notes seven blessings that came to Abraham through this trial of his faith.[1] First, the trial was withdrawn and Isaac was unharmed. Second, Abraham received the highest approval of God for not withholding anything from Him. Third, Abraham saw God in a new light, as one who would be willing to sacrifice His own Son, Jesus, for the sins of us all. Fourth, more of God's nature was revealed. He became known as Jehovah Jireh, the God who provides. Fifth, God confirmed his covenant with Abraham because Abraham proved himself faithful at all costs. Sixth, God reemphasized his promise to Abraham about his offspring. "I will surely bless you and make your descendants as numerous as the stars in the sky and as the sand on the seashore" (Gen. 22:17). And finally, God gave Abraham a distinct and personal blessing that has never been repeated.

And through your offspring all nations on earth will be blessed, because you have obeyed me.

—GENESIS 22:18

Imagine Abraham's joy as he came down the mountain with Isaac. His soul must have been filled with exultation, triumph, praise, and glory. God did it! God is faithful! Hallelujah! Abraham must have been overwhelmed and full of joy—the joy of worshiping Jehovah Jireh, the God who provides. Abraham did not have to offer his son. The Lord was his provider.

In the same way we must abandon ourselves to God in every circumstance. We must believe in the Jireh half of the Lord's name, Jehovah-Jireh. We must believe that the Lord will provide everything!

> When the LORD brought back the captives to Zion, we were like men who dreamed. Our mouths were filled with laughter, our tongues with songs of joy. Then it was said among the nations, "The LORD has done great things for them." The LORD has done great things for us, and we are filled with joy.
> —PSALM 126:1–3

This is the joy of abandoned faith. Abraham went up Mount Moriah filled with faith. He ran down the mountain overwhelmed with joy. We can approach the mountains of our own experiences in the same way: up with faith in our hearts, and back down filled with joy.

Recently I was given a copy of a beautiful sermon by C. H. Spurgeon that is more than one hundred years old. It was based on Romans 15:13:

> May the God of hope fill you with all joy and peace as you trust in him, so that you may overflow with hope by the power of the Holy Spirit.

I love how Spurgeon then tied peace and joy together. He said, "Peace is joy resting, and joy is peace dancing. Joy cries 'Hosannah' before the well-beloved, but peace leans her head on His bosom." Peace and joy balance beautifully because they balance on Calvary. There is nothing we can do to force that balance. We must be centered on Christ and Calvary, having faith in Him and not in ourselves.

Two things we see constantly in the early Christians are the love of Christ and joy in Christ. They gave up all their material things, renounced everything that was dear to them, and faced all kinds of suffering.

What happened? Well, the world thought they were crazy. They were imprisoned, tortured, and killed. But that did not stop others from carrying on the mission. The flame of God's truth kept burning brightly.

These early believers had unspeakable joy. They loved God so much that they no longer saw with physical eyes. The pearls of God's majesty were transformed into their eyes, and they saw as God saw, not as the world saw. They saw something unseen—heaven, eternity. They loved Jesus Christ because they saw Him spiritually, and the world saw Him not.

> Though you have not seen him, you love him; and even though you do not see him now, you believe in him and are filled with an inexpressible and glorious joy, for you are receiving the goal of your faith, the salvation of your souls.
>
> —1 PETER 1:8–9

Like them, we can experience a transforming encounter in God's joy and majesty when we fix our hearts and eyes on Him. We can see like He sees, and our hearts can feel like He feels. We can worship Him and become connected to His love and joy. Then we have true union and communion with God—in thanksgiving, prayer, service, felicity, rejoicing, and praise.

BELIEVE, THEN WE WILL BE ENABLED TO REJOICE

When we truly believe, then we will be able to rejoice with joy both inexpressible and full of glory. True faith is receiving God's Word and resting in His redemption. True faith is hearing the Bible, not as the word of man, but as the Word of God. It is experiencing the reality of Jesus' words:

> My sheep hear My voice, and I know them, and they follow Me.
>
> —JOHN 10:27, NKJV

True faith is person-to-person dealing with God. Nothing is more empty than to have a superficial pretense of believing God, to not really have faith as the greatest passion of our heart. True faith includes a humility and repentance that receives Jesus' benediction poured out upon our heads and in our hearts:

> Blessed are the poor in spirit, For theirs is the kingdom of heaven.
> Blessed are those who mourn, For they shall be comforted.
>
> —MATTHEW 5:3–4, NKJV

When we believe God's promises from the depth of our hearts the things that God promises become ours. We are forgiven and can hear Him say to us as He did to the man let down through the roof at Jesus' feet:

> Son, be of good cheer; your sins are forgiven you.
>
> —MATTHEW 9:2, NKJV

True faith is an inquiring soul that asks, "Lord, do you care for lepers? Are you willing to cleanse them?" Jesus answers, "I am willing; be cleansed." By faith we possess the promises of God and their fulfillments. The broadest, most encompassing promise of all is:

> I will be a Father to you, and you shall be My sons and daughters, says the LORD Almighty.
>
> —2 CORINTHIANS 6:18, NKJV

This is the same as God saying to Abraham:

> I am your shield, your exceedingly great reward.
>
> —GENESIS 15:1, NKJV

We can say like Jeremiah, "The LORD is my portion"(Lam. 3:24). Faith hears God say to the soul out of His Word by the power of the Holy Spirit, "I will never leave you, nor forsake you. I have loved you with an everlasting love. Fear not, for I am with you." Is it any wonder that joy now fills the heart and floods the soul? When we truly drink these promises in and believe them as true for ourselves then we will rejoice. This is the order: believe and rejoice. Believe and then you will truly rejoice. We are promised a joy that the world cannot give and the world cannot take away. We are enabled to "rejoice in the Lord always. I will say it again: Rejoice" (Phil. 4:4) because the forgiveness and new life that we have in the Savior is from Him and cannot be taken away by any trial or difficulty. However, we must believe Him. We must see Him above all things ruling and reigning, and trust His sovereignty to work all things for good for those who love Him. Then we can continue to say, "The joy of the Lord is my strength."

Let us believe, and then we will be able to rejoice. May we believe until we rejoice. Lord, sustain our faith and strengthen our joy!

VERSES ABOUT JOY

H ERE are some verses from God's Word to help us rejoice in the Lord and in His joy.

Glory in his holy name; let the hearts of those who seek the LORD rejoice.

—1 CHRONICLES 16:10

You have made known to me the path of life; you will fill me with joy in your presence, with eternal pleasures at your right hand.

—PSALM 16:11

The LORD is my light and my salvation—whom shall I fear? the LORD is the stronghold of my life—of whom shall I be afraid?

—PSALM 27:1

You turned my wailing into dancing; you removed my sackcloth and clothed me with joy.

—PSALM 30:11

Then my soul will rejoice in the LORD and delight in his salvation.

—PSALM 35:9

But may all who seek you rejoice and be glad in you; may those who love your salvation always say, "The LORD be exalted!"

—PSALM 40:16

Then I will go to the altar of God, to God, my joy and my delight. I will praise you with the harp, O God, my God.

—PSALM 43:4

Create in me a pure heart, O God, and renew a steadfast spirit within me. Do not cast me from your presence or take your Holy Spirit from me. Restore to me the joy of your salvation and grant me a willing spirit, to sustain me.

—PSALM 51:10–12

Blessed are those who have learned to acclaim you, who walk in the light of your presence, O LORD. They rejoice in your name all day long; they exult in your righteousness.

—PSALM 89:15–16

The LORD your God is with you, he is mighty to save. He will take great delight in you, he will quiet you with his love, he will rejoice over you with singing.

—ZEPHANIAH 3:17

Therefore we do not lose heart. Though outwardly we are wasting away, yet inwardly we are being renewed day by day. For our light and momentary troubles are achieving for us an eternal glory that far outweighs them all. So we fix our eyes not on what is seen, but on what is unseen. For what is seen is temporary, but what is unseen is eternal.

—2 CORINTHIANS 4:16–18

That Christ may dwell in your hearts through faith. And I pray that you, being rooted and established in love, may have power, together with all the saints, to grasp how wide and long and high and deep is the love of Christ, and to know this love that surpasses knowledge—that you may be filled to the measure of all the fullness of God.

—EPHESIANS 3:17–19

Rejoice in the Lord always. I will say it again: Rejoice!

—PHILIPPIANS 4:4

Do not be anxious about anything, but in everything, by prayer and petition, with thanksgiving, present your requests to God. And the peace of God, which transcends all understanding, will guard your hearts and your minds in Christ Jesus.

—PHILIPPIANS 4:6–7

Finally, brothers, whatever is true, whatever is noble, whatever is right, whatever is pure, whatever is lovely, whatever is admirable—if anything is excellent or praiseworthy—think about such things. Whatever you have learned or received or heard from me, or seen in me—put it into practice. And the God of peace will be with you.

—PHILIPPIANS 4:8–9

Be joyful always; pray continually; give thanks in all circumstances, for this is God's will for you in Christ Jesus.

—1 THESSALONIANS 5:16–18

VERSES ABOUT WORSHIP

ERE are some verses from God's Word to give us greater insight in worshiping the Lord.

Do not worship any other god, for the LORD, whose name is Jealous, is a jealous God.

—EXODUS 34:14

Love the LORD your God with all your heart and with all your soul and with all your strength.

—DEUTERONOMY 6:5

Glory in his holy name; let the hearts of those who seek the LORD rejoice.

—1 CHRONICLES 16:10

Yours, O LORD, is the greatness and the power and the glory and the majesty and the splendor, for everything in heaven and earth is yours. Yours, O LORD, is the kingdom; you are exalted as head over all.

—1 CHRONICLES 29:11

I will praise you, O LORD, with all my heart; I will tell of all your wonders.

—PSALM 9:1

The heavens declare the glory of God; the skies proclaim the work of his hands.

—PSALM 19:1

Many, O LORD my God, are the wonders you have done. The things you planned for us no one can recount to you; were I to speak and tell of them, they would be too many to declare.

—PSALM 40:5

As the deer pants for streams of water so my soul pants for you, O God. My soul thirsts for God, for the living God. When can I go and meet with God?

—PSALM 42:1–2

Then I will go to the altar of God, to God, my joy and my delight. I will praise you with the harp, O God, my God.

—PSALM 43:4

Whom have I in heaven but you? And earth has nothing I desire besides you. My flesh and my heart may fail, but God is the strength of my heart and my portion forever.

—PSALM 73:25-26

Look to the LORD and his strength; seek his face always.

—PSALM 105:4

Therefore, I urge you, brothers, in view of God's mercy, to offer your bodies as living sacrifices, holy and pleasing to God—this is your spiritual act of worship.

—ROMANS 12:1

That Christ may dwell in your hearts through faith. And I pray that you, being rooted and established in love, may have power, together with all the saints, to grasp how wide and long and high and deep is the love of Christ, and to know this love that surpasses knowledge—that you may be filled to the measure of all the fullness of God.

—EPHESIANS 3:17–19

Finally, brothers, whatever is true, whatever is noble, whatever is right, whatever is pure, whatever is lovely, whatever is admirable—if anything is excellent or praiseworthy—think about such things. Whatever you have learned or received or heard from me, or seen in me—put it into practice. And the God of peace will be with you.

—PHILIPPIANS 4:8–9

RELINQUISHED HEART OR RELIGIOUS SPIRIT?

H ERE are some verses that outline the difference between a relinquished heart and a religious spirit.

FOUNDATION OF THE RELINQUISHED HEART: THE ROOTS OF JOY

The relinquished heart is surrendered to Christ:

> I have been crucified with Christ and I no longer live, but Christ lives in me.
>
> —GALATIANS 2:20

The religious heart is independent:

> Trust in the LORD with all your heart and lean not on your own understanding; in all your ways acknowledge him, and he will make your paths straight.
>
> —PROVERBS 3:5–6

The relinquished heart is repentant:

> The sacrifices of God are a broken spirit; a broken and contrite heart, O God, you will not despise.
>
> —PSALM 51:17

The religious spirit is overconfident and proud:

> So, if you think you are standing firm, be careful that you don't fall!
>
> —1 CORINTHIANS 10:12

FOCUS OF THE RELINQUISHED HEART: GOD IS THE SOURCE OF JOY

The relinquished heart is God-centered:

> I have set the LORD always before me. Because he is at my right hand, I will not be shaken.
>
> —PSALM 16:8

The religious spirit is self-centered:

> Stop trusting in man, who has but a breath in his nostrils. Of what account is he?
>
> —ISAIAH 2:22

The relinquished heart genuinely praises God:

> I will praise the LORD all my life; I will sing praise to my God as long as I live.
>
> —PSALM 146:2

The religious spirit pays God lip service:

> "These people honor me with their lips, but their hearts are far from me. They worship me in vain; their teachings are but rules taught by men."
>
> —MATTHEW 15:8–9

The relinquished heart has an eternal view:

> Therefore we do not lose heart. Though outwardly we are
> wasting away, yet inwardly we are being renewed day by day.
> For our light and momentary troubles are achieving for us an
> eternal glory that far outweighs them all. So we fix our eyes
> not on what is seen, but on what is unseen. For what is seen is
> temporary, but what is unseen is eternal.
>
> —2 CORINTHIANS 4:16–18

The religious spirit is temporal:

> Why, you do not even know what will happen tomorrow. What
> is your life? You are a mist that appears for a little while and
> then vanishes.
>
> —JAMES 4:14

The relinquished heart follows the major commandment:

> Love the LORD your God with all your heart and with all your
> soul and with all your strength.
>
> —DEUTERONOMY 6:5

The religious spirit is busy following minor rules:

> Woe to you, teachers of the law and Pharisees, you hypocrites!
> You give a tenth [as your tithe]…But you have neglected the
> more important matters of the law—justice, mercy and faith-
> fulness. You should have practiced the latter, without neglecting
> the former.
>
> —MATTHEW 23:23

The relinquished heart is aligned to God:

> Though you have not seen him, you love him; and even though
> you do not see him now, you believe in him and are filled with
> an inexpressible and glorious joy.
>
> —1 PETER 1:8

The religious spirit is aligned to the world:

> Don't you know that friendship with the world is hatred toward
> God? Anyone who chooses to be a friend of the world becomes
> an enemy of God.
>
> —James 4:4

Freedom of the Relinquished Heart: By the Holy Spirit, the Power of Joy

The relinquished heart is set on internal attitudes:

> Set your minds on things above, not on earthly things. For you
> died, and your life is now hidden with Christ in God.
>
> —Colossians 3:2–3

The religious spirit is set on external actions:

> Since you died with Christ to the basic principles of this world,
> why, as though you still belonged to it, do you submit to its
> rules: "Do not handle! Do not taste! Do not touch!" These
> are all destined to perish with use, because they are based on
> human commands and teachings.
>
> —Colossians 2:20–22

In the relinquished heart, peace is joy resting and joy is peace dancing:

> May the God of hope fill you with all joy and peace as you trust
> in him, so that you may overflow with hope by the power of
> the Holy Spirit.
>
> —Romans 15:13

In the religious spirit, there is false peace and no joy:

> 'Peace, peace,' they say, when there is no peace.
>
> —Jeremiah 6:14

Fruit of the Relinquished Heart: Experiences and Expressions of Joy

The relinquished heart is humble:

> All of you, clothe yourselves with humility toward one another, because, "God opposes the proud but gives grace to the humble." Humble yourselves, therefore, under God's mighty hand, that he may lift you up in due time.
>
> —1 Peter 5:5–6

The religious spirit is full of false pride:

> Do not keep talking so proudly or let your mouth speak such arrogance, for the Lord is a God who knows, and by him deeds are weighed.
>
> —1 Samuel 2:3

The relinquished heart is filled with life through the fruit of the Holy Spirit:

> But the fruit of the Spirit is love, joy, peace, patience, kindness, goodness, faithfulness, gentleness and self-control. Against such things there is no law.
>
> —Galatians 5:22–23

The religious spirit is killed by legalism:

> He has made us competent as ministers of a new covenant—not of the letter [or law] but of the Spirit; for the letter kills, but the Spirit gives life.
>
> —2 Corinthians 3:6

The relinquished heart is patient:

> Be still before the Lord and wait patiently for him; do not fret when men succeed in their ways, when they carry out their wicked schemes.
>
> —Psalm 37:7

The religious spirit is strangled by worry:

> But the worries of this life, the deceitfulness of wealth and the
> desires for other things come in and choke the word, making
> it unfruitful.
>
> —MARK 4:19

The relinquished heart intercedes for others:

> Therefore confess your sins to each other and pray for each
> other so that you may be healed.
>
> —JAMES 5:16

The religious spirit accuses and criticizes:

> If you keep on biting and devouring each other, watch out or
> you will be destroyed by each other.
>
> —GALATIANS 5:15

The relinquished heart puts others first:

> Do nothing out of selfish ambition or vain conceit, but in
> humility consider others better than yourselves. Each of you
> should look not only to your own interests, but also to the
> interests of others.
>
> —PHILIPPIANS 2:3–4

The religious spirit is full of self-importance:

> If anyone thinks he is something when he is nothing, he
> deceives himself.
>
> —GALATIANS 6:3

FUEL (MOTIVES) OF THE RELINQUISHED HEART: RENEWING OF JOY

The relinquished heart longs for the Word of God:

> My soul is consumed with longing for your laws at all times.
>
> —PSALM 119:20

The religious spirit is complacent and smug:

> He who is full loathes honey, but to the hungry even what is
> bitter tastes sweet.
>
> —PROVERBS 27:7

The relinquished heart prays with the Holy Spirit:

> I pray that out of his glorious riches he may strengthen you with
> power through his Spirit in your inner being.
>
> —EPHESIANS 3:16

The religious spirit uses formal prayer:

> These people honor me with their lips, but their hearts are far
> from me.
>
> —MATTHEW 15:8

FIRE OF THE RELINQUISHED HEART: MAJESTY OF JOY, THE ULTIMATE JOY

The relinquished heart is filled with God's presence:

> You have made known to me the path of life; you will fill me
> with joy in your presence, with eternal pleasures at your right
> hand.
>
> —PSALM 16:11

The religious spirit knows only cold obedience, the opposite of love:

> "If you love me, you will obey what I command."
>
> —JOHN 14:15

SCRIPTURE INDEX

Acts 3:19 *56*
Acts 13:52 *21*
Acts 17:24–28 *59*
1 Chronicles 16:10 *5, 81, 85*
1 Chronicles 29:11 *62, 86*
2 Chronicles 7:14 *55*
2 Chronicles 14:11 *34*
2 Chronicles 16:9 *34*
Colossians 2:20–22 *49, 92*
1 Corinthians 13 *14*
1 Corinthians 15:31 *15*
2 Corinthians 3:6 *49, 93*
2 Corinthians 3:18 *67*
2 Corinthians 4:6 *20*
2 Corinthians 4:10 *15*
2 Corinthians 4:16–18 *41, 82, 91*
Daniel 4:37 *40*
Deuteronomy 6:5 *13, 85, 91*
Ephesians 2:8–9 *10*

Ephesians 2:10 *64*
Ephesians 3:17–19 *2, 66, 83, 87*
Exodus 34:14 *61, 85*
Exodus 34:29–31, 33–35 *20*
Galatians 2:20 *6, 15, 16, 27, 31, 89*
Galatians 5:22–23 *27, 93*
Galatians 6:3 *73, 94*
Genesis 2:23 *14*
Genesis 22:9–12 *76*
Genesis 22:17 *76*
Genesis 22:18 *76*
Genesis 31:32 *44*
Hebrews 2:7 *63*
Hebrews 11:17–19 *76*
Isaiah 2:22 *28, 90*
James 4:4 *16, 92*
James 4:14 *28, 91*
John 1:4 *20*

97

John 4:32, 34 66
John 12:24–25 15
1 John 1:3–4 19
1 John 1:9 55
Jeremiah 15:19 55
Luke 9:23–24 15
Luke 10:41–42 37
Luke 15:21 54
Luke 15:23 54
Luke 16:19–26 39
Mark 4:19 38, 94
Matthew 5:14–16 73
Matthew 15:8–9 47, 90, 95
Matthew 22:37, 39 62
Matthew 23:23 50, 91
Philippians 2:3–4 74, 94
Philippians 2:5–8 31
Philippians 3:8–9 16
Philippians 4:4 70, 83
Philippians 4:6–7 30, 83
Philippians 4:8–9 71, 83, 87
1 Peter 1:8 78, 91
1 Peter 5:5–6 49, 93
Proverbs 3:5 29, 89
Proverbs 13:12 36
Proverbs 14:30 38
Proverbs 28:13 54
Psalm 9:1 59, 86
Psalm 16:8 47, 90

Psalm 16:11 67, 69, 81, 95
Psalm 19:1 58, 86
Psalm 27:1 31, 81
Psalm 30:11 36, 81
Psalm 35:9 11, 82
Psalm 40:5 57, 86
Psalm 40:16 68, 82
Psalm 42:1–2 50, 86
Psalm 43:4 60, 82, 86
Psalm 51:10–12 53, 82
Psalm 51:17 56, 90
Psalm 73:25–26 2, 28, 86
Psalm 89:15–16 57, 82
Psalm 100:2 74
Psalm 105:4 48, 86
Psalm 126:1–3 77
Psalm 149:4 7
Romans 10:17 17
Romans 12:1 65, 87
Romans 12:2 28
Romans 14:23 55
Romans 15:13 22, 77, 92
1 Samuel 2:3 48, 93
1 Samuel 4 46
1 Samuel 25:29 51
1 Thessalonians 5:16–18 83
Titus 2:14 56
Zephaniah 3:17 9, 82

NOTES

INTRODUCTION

1. Henry Scougal, *The Life of God in the Soul of Man* (Harrisonburg, VA: Sprinkle Publications, 1986).

CHAPTER 1
A HEART OF FAITH, A LIFE OF JOY

1. C. S. Lewis, *Surprised by Joy* (Orlando, FL: Harcourt Brace, 1956).

2. C. S. Lewis, *The Weight of Glory and Other Addresses* (Grand Rapids, MI: William B. Eerdmans Publishing Co., 1965).

CHAPTER 2
THE JOY OF SALVATION

1. Jonathan Edwards. *The Works of Jonathan Edwards* (Edinburgh: Banner of Truth Trust, 1974).

CHAPTER 3
BEING RELINQUISHED

1. Charles Swindoll, *Laugh Again* (Dallas, TX: Word Books, 1992).

2. Owen Milton, *Christian Missionaries* (Bryntirion, Wales; Evangelical Press, 1995) 69.

3. C. H. Spurgeon, *Autobiography* (Edinburgh: Banner of Truth Trust, 1962).

4. Tony Evans, *The Fire That Ignites* (Sisters, OR: Multnomah Publishers, 2003), 10.

CHAPTER 4
TRAITS OF A RELINQUISHED LIFE

1. Earl Palmer, *The Search for Joy*, April 23, 1995, found at www.30goodminutes.org/cses/sermon/palmer (accessed June 8, 2004).

CHAPTER 6
RELINQUISHED OR RELIGIOUS?

1. Martyn Lloyd-Jones, *Spiritual Depression: Its Causes and Cure* (Grand Rapids, MI: William B. Eerdmans Publishing Co, 1965).

CHAPTER 8
WORSHIP AND JOY

1. John Piper, *Desiring God: Meditations of a Christian Hedonist* (Portland, OR: Multnomah Press, 1991).

2. Jonathan Edwards, *The Works of Jonathan Edwards*, vol. 1 (Carlisle, PA: The Banner of Truth Trust, 1990).

3. Ibid.

4. Ibid.

5. Chuck Colson, Prison Fellowship Ministry, 1856 Old Reston Ave., Reston, VA 20190, email: correspondence@pfm.org.

6. John Piper, *Desiring God: Meditations of a Christian Hedonist* (Portland, OR: Multnomah Press, 1991) and *The Pleasures of God: Meditations on God's Delight in Being God* (Portland, OR: Multnomah Press, 1991).

7. Henry Scougal, *The Life of God in the Soul of Man* (Harrisonburg, VA: Sprinkle Publications, 1986).

8. Nigel Clifford, *Christian Preachers* ((Bryntirion, Wales; Evangelical Press, 1994) 161.

9. *The Westminster Larger Catechism*, 2002, found at www.reformed. org/document/larger1.html (accessed June 1, 2004).

CHAPTER 9
A JOYOUS LIFE

1. C. S. Lewis, *Surprised by Joy* (Orlando, FL: Harcourt Brace, 1956).

2. Paraphrased from *The Works of Jonathan Edwards*, Vol. 1 (Carlisle, PA: The Banner of Truth Trust, 1990).

3. *The Works of Jonathan Edwards*, Vol. 1 (Carlisle, PA: The Banner of Truth Trust, 1990).

4. Ibid.

CHAPTER 10
JOY AND PEACE

1. C. H. Spurgeon, *Autobiography* (Edinburgh: Banner of Truth Trust, 1962).

ABOUT THE AUTHOR

James P. Gills, M.D., is founder and director of St. Luke's Cataract and Laser Institute in Tarpon Springs, Florida. Internationally respected as a cataract surgeon, Dr. Gills has performed more cataract extractions with lens implantations than anyone else in the world. He has pioneered many advancements in the field of ophthalmology to make cataract surgery safer and easier.

As a world-renowned ophthalmologist, Dr. Gills has received innumerable medical and educational awards, highlighted by 1994–2004 listings in *The Best Doctors in America*. Dr. Gills is a clinical professor of ophthalmology at The University of South Florida, and was named one of the Best Ophthalmologists in America in 1996 by ophthalmic academic leaders nationwide. He has served on the Board of Directors of the American College of Eye Surgeons, the Board of Visitors at Duke University Medical Center, and the Advisory Board of Wilmer Ophthalmological Institute at Johns Hopkins University. He has published more than 185 medical papers and authored nine medical textbooks. Listed in Marquis' *Who's Who in America*, Dr. Gills was Entrepreneur of the Year 1990 for the State of Florida, received the Tampa Bay Business Hall of Fame Award in 1993 and the Tampa Bay Ethics Award from the University of Tampa in 1995. In 1996 he was awarded the prestigious Innovators Award by his colleagues in the American Society of Cataract and Refractive Surgeons. In 2000 he was presented with the Florida Enterprise Medal by the Merchants Association of Florida, named Humanitarian of the Year by the Golda Meir/Kent Jewish Center in Clearwater, and Free Enterpriser of the Year by the Florida Council on Economic Education. In 2001 The Salvation Army presented Dr. Gills their prestigious "Others" Award in honor of his lifelong commitment to service and caring.

Virginia Polytechnic Institute, Dr. Gills' alma mater, presented their University Distinguished Achievement Award to him in 2003. In that same year, Dr. Gills was appointed by Governor Jeb Bush to the Board of Directors of the Florida Sports Foundation. In 2004 Dr. Gills was invited to join the prestigious Florida Council of 100, an advisory committee reporting directly to the governor on various aspects of Florida public policy affecting the quality of life and economic well-being of all Floridians.

While Dr. Gills has many accomplishments and varied interests, his primary focus is to restore physical vision to patients and bring spiritual enlightenment through his life. Guided by his strong and enduring faith in Jesus Christ, he seeks to encourage and comfort the patients who come to St. Luke's and to share his faith whenever possible. It was through sharing his insights with patients that he initially began writing on Christian topics. An avid student of the Bible for many years, he now has authored seventeen books on Christian living, with over five million in print. With the exception of the Bible, Dr. Gills' books are the most widely requested books in the U.S. prison system. In addition, Dr. Gills has published more than 185 medical articles and authored or coauthored nine medical reference textbooks. Five of those books were best-sellers at the American Academy of Ophthalmology annual meetings.

As an ultra-distance athlete, Dr. Gills participated in forty-six marathons, including eighteen Boston Marathons and fourteen 100-mile mountain runs. In addition, he completed five Ironman Triathlons in Hawaii and six Double Iron Triathlons. Dr. Gills has served on the National Board of Directors of the Fellowship of Christian Athletes and in 1991 was the first recipient of their Tom Landry Award.

Married in 1962, Dr. Gills and his wife, Heather, have raised two children, Shea and Pit. Shea Gills Grundy, a former attorney now full-time mom, is a graduate of Vanderbilt University and Emory University Law School. She and husband Shane Grundy, M.D. presented the Gills with their first grandchildren—twins, Maggie and Braddock.

They have since been joined by Jimmy Gills and Lily Grace. The Gills' son, J. Pit Gills, M.D., ophthalmologist, received his medical degree from Duke University Medical Center and in 2001 joined the St. Luke's staff. "Dr. Pit" and his wife, Joy, are the proud parents of Pitzer and Parker.

OTHER MATERIALS BY JAMES P. GILLS, M.D.

DARWINISM UNDER THE MICROSCOPE: HOW RECENT SCIENTIFIC
EVIDENCE POINTS TO DIVINE DESIGN
(coauthored with Tom Woodward, Ph.D.)
Read about the truth of creation that your science texts have been avoiding.
ISBN 0-88419-925-8

GOD'S PRESCRIPTION FOR HEALING: FIVE DIVINE GIFTS OF HEALING
Grow in wonder and appreciation of God as you read about His five divine
gifts of healing to us.
ISBN 1-59185-286-2

IMAGINATIONS: MORE THAN YOU THINK
This book shows how focusing our thoughts will help us grow closer to God.
ISBN 1-59185-609-4

RX FOR WORRY: A THANKFUL HEART
Dr. Gills shows how each of us can find peace by resting and rejoicing in the
promises of God.
ISBN 0-88419-932-0

SPIRITUAL BLINDNESS: DEPENDING ON GOD, ABIDING IN TRUE FAITH
Jesus + anything = nothing. Jesus + nothing = everything. Here is a book that
will help you recognize the spiritual blindness in all of us and fulfill the Lord's
plan for you.
ISBN 1-59185-607-8

THE DYNAMICS OF WORSHIP: LOVING GOD THROUGH GENUINE
WORSHIP
Designed to rekindle the heart with a passionate love for God, it gives the
who, what, when, where, why, and how of worship.
ISBN 1-59185-657-4

THE PRAYERFUL SPIRIT: PASSION FOR GOD, COMPASSION FOR PEOPLE
This book tells how prayer has changed Dr. Gills' life, as well as the lives of
patients and other doctors.
ISBN 1-59185-215-3

COME UNTO ME: GOD'S CALL TO INTIMACY
Inspired by Dr. Gills' trip to the Holy Land, it explores God's eternal desire for mankind to get to know Him intimately.

ISBN 1-59185-214-5

TEMPLE MAINTENANCE: EXCELLENCE WITH LOVE
A how-to book for achieving lifelong total fitness of body, mind, and spirit.

ISBN 1-879938-01-4

LOVE: FULFILLING THE ULTIMATE QUEST
A quick refresher course on the meaning and method of God's great gift.

ISBN 0-88419-933-9

THE UNSEEN ESSENTIAL: A STORY FOR OUR TROUBLED TIMES
A compelling, contemporary novel about one man's struggle to grow into God's kind of love.

ISBN 1-879938-05-7

TENDER JOURNEY: A CONTINUING STORY FOR OUR TROUBLED TIMES
The popular sequel to *The Unseen Essential.*

ISBN 1-879938-17-0

A BIBLICAL ECONOMICS MANIFESTO: ECONOMICS AND THE CHRISTIAN WORLDVIEW
(coauthored with Ronald H. Nash, Ph.D.)
Money and economics are necessities of life; read what the Bible has to say about them.

ISBN 0-88419-871-5

THE WORRY DISEASE
A colorful 4- by 8.5-inch pamphlet on the most common disease.

TRANSFORM YOUR MARRIAGE
An elegant 4- by 8.5-inch booklet to help couples develop new closeness with each other and with the Lord.

ISBN 1-879938-11-1

DID YOU ENJOY
THIS BOOK?

Dr. and Mrs. James P. Gills would love to hear from you! Please let them know if *Believe and Rejoice* has had an effect in your life or in the lives of your loved ones. Send your letters to:

St. Luke's Cataract and Laser Institute
P.O. Box 5000
Tarpon Springs, FL 34688-5000
Telephone: (727) 938-2020, Ext. 2200
(800) 282-9905, Ext. 2200
Fax: (727) 372-3605